Life From the
Stoop

Elizabeth Mejia

Life From The Stoop
Copyright © 2012 by Elizabeth Mejia

The names and identification of some characters in this book have been changed.

ISBN-13: 978-1475039184
ISBN-10: 1475039182

1. Memoir 2. Puerto Rican 3. Inspirational 4. Alcoholism 5. Domestic Violence

Order books at: https://www.createspace.com/3825238

Dedication

TO MY MOTHER, Elizabeth Garcia, who showered me with much love and gave me the greatest gift a mother can give: her faith in God and her unconditional love. I also dedicate this book to my brother and sisters, who shared this journey with me.

Acknowledgements

I WOULD LIKE to thank my husband, Francisco Mejia, and my daughters, Elyssa and Raquel, for their support and encouragement, especially Elyssa for critiquing my work and pushing me to deeper levels.

A very special thank you goes to my sisters and brother for sharing and encouraging me despite the difficult memories. I most especially thank my sister, Silvia Jobbagy, for her contributions.

Several special people helped in providing me guidance, support, insights, editing, and encouragement. I thank them all for their invaluable support, especially Maritza Ascorbe and Christina Monteanu.

Introduction

FOR YEARS I'VE wanted to write about my childhood. But instead of writing my story, I've shared it as a motivational speaker to women and youth. I felt if I wrote about my family, it might dishonor them. This was enough to result in several false starts, and eventually the desire to record my life story languished.

Now as a 50-year old grandmother, I think of how much of my family history is already lost. Without a strong, extended family with intergenerational members represented, our oral history has died. I cherish the stories on my husband's side. But to hear their stories repeated and enjoyed time and time again also saddens me because my side of the family can't share a similar experience. Over the years, our family tree has begun to wither to a few branches and leaves. This was enough to finally propel me to just begin to write.

I write first and foremost for my family. It is my aim to honor the memory of my father, mother, and the truth of how we lived and survived. I acknowledge that as a memoir, it is solely based on my personal memories and feelings from my various life stages and perspective at the time, and most likely one-sided information. Despite what I share about our most personal family stories, it is not meant to dishonor my mother whom I love and cherish. If there is one thing I know is that people are very complex. No one is one-dimensional. I realize I can never represent my mother in the fullness of who she truly was. My siblings have been very understanding and supportive, and I'm grateful to them for sharing their memories to help me write our story. I leave this memoir as a gift to my grandchildren. I want them to know who I was, how I grew up, and how I survived a chaotic past. I also leave this for my nephews and nieces. I love them so much and yet strangers in an audience have learned more about my history than they have. After all, how could I introduce my story to them? There was never a context for it over dinner or a family gathering. So this is for them as well.

Lastly, I hope that my life story touches others. In this memoir, I write that "I ran away and never looked back." That's not entirely accurate. I've always looked back to who I was, where I came from, and how it shaped me. My entire professional career has been devoted to helping women and children. My story hopefully touches women and young people who are struggling in poverty, alcohol and substance abuse, domestic violence, destructive relationships, and other forms of life-choking despair. To them I state the obvious: change always comes. With change there is great reason to hold on to hope. My faith in God has been my strength, and I believe that hope is the greatest gift that our Lord has given us. I've prayed to Him in my time of need and have learned to trust in His wisdom and love. I hope my readers will find comfort in the same.

Papi Que Se Murio

"*MAMI CAME RUNNING* and poured a bucket of water on my face," laughed my husband, Frank, as he shared the story of when his younger brother tried to flip him and his head crashed onto the floor. His boisterous and contagious laughter has everyone laughing as heartily as if it was the first time they have ever heard this beloved family tale.

We are all gathered in my kitchen, well sated from a dinner of *arroz con pollo* (rice with chicken), yet eagerly digging into the birthday cake for my *suegro* (father in-law). Birthday dinners are a great Mejia tradition which brings everyone together from our 104 year old great aunt, Graciela, to the youngest newborn, Nicolas. Four generations of Mejia, easily over 22 people, laughing, dancing, eating, and re-telling family stories.

I move to the living room and there are my daughters, Elyssa and Raquel, pouring over family pictures, their favorite pastime. "Oh my gosh, remember this?" Raquel squeals yet again as she passes the album to her cousins. Contentment brings a smile to my face, as I wait for the familiar threats of which picture they will project at each other's wedding as a weapon of embarrassment.

After 29-years of marriage you would think these scenes will become mundane, instead they fill me with great joy and moments to treasure. Even the youngest, my four year old granddaughter, lovingly adds her two cents, "I miss my *bisabuela* (great grandmother)," someone she has never met.

Amidst the laughter and good humor, I feel a twinge of sadness mixed with a deep sense of gratitude. As I look at Elyssa and Raquel, I'm transported back to my old orange sofa, with its sticky plastic protective cover, where I similarly sat with my sister Silvia looking at old family albums.

"Look how handsome *papi que se murió* is," I point to Silvia as we sit looking at pictures. Not noticing how peculiar it is to refer to my father as *papi que se murio* (daddy that died).

"That's not him," corrects Silvia.

"I know, but I bet he looked like that," I reply.

"This is my favorite; I think he looks more like him," shares Silvia, speculating further because we have no pictures or recollections of him.

Unlike my girls who have always had the security of having an involved, loving father in their life, I didn't. I was only two years old when he died.

My girls have the pleasure of being "daddy's girls," being someone's princess, being spoiled and most importantly feeling protected. Frank will do anything for his girls. He fills any of their whims and needs, providing tremendous security to them and rushing to their rescue in whatever they need.

In contrast, I have a void. I have no memories of him whatsoever. I'm only left with stories; stories that I'm sure did not capture the fullness of the man. I grew up wondering how it would feel to have a father. I looked at other fathers with their children, swinging them onto their shoulders. The children would be giggling and happy, enjoying that age-old special bond between children and fathers. Envy would pierce through me like a swift blade causing instant pain, yearning for those moments where I was the one being thrown around on my father's strong shoulders. It looked like fun.

Then again, I'd also see the stern fathers, removed from their children – unapproachable. These fathers were cold, hard, and even abusive. I remember one of my neighbors whose father sexually molested her and her sisters. In those moments, a great sense of relief washed over me.

"Aha," I would rationalize "how lucky I am not to have a father after all."

But the main sentiment I had was curiosity. What if he lived? What would my life be like? This unanswerable question led to hours of daydreams and possibilities. As a science fiction fan, I think of parallel dimensions. Who would I be if he had just lived? How would my mother's life been different? Empty questions – are they not? I am who I am because he did die. So how did his death mold me?

Before I go there, let me introduce you to Pedro Garcia, better known as Pellin, or simply *papi que se murio*.

Papi que se murio came to the United States when he was around 15 years old. He ventured out from Puerto Rico with his uncle looking for a better life in America. The rest of his family subsequently joined him, and they moved from New Jersey to Connecticut. When he met my mother, he relentlessly pursued her. Initially, she resisted him finding him to be conceited and overly proud. Undeterred, he announced that he would make her his wife. Sure enough, they fell in love and eloped.

My father in one word was a hero, a documented, certified hero. The newspaper headlines proclaimed, "He Died for Decency."

It was a warm fall evening, October 9, 1963. After a long shift at the Coca-Cola Bottling Company, my father with my uncle Pablo left work at 11:30 p.m. As they approached their car, a noise drew *papi's que se murio's* attention.

"Hey look, look over there," he pointed towards the loading dock to my uncle. "It looks like they're stealing! We have to do something," he exclaimed as he, without any hesitation, started to rush in that direction.

Pablo grabbed his arm, "No, let's go; forget it man."

"No way, we could scare them away," my father said as he hurried away to confront the thieves.

"Damn, Pellin, come back," whispered Pablo as he saw the back of my father run towards the dock. He stood back conflicted, not wanting to get involved. The decision, however, was quickly made for him, when he heard a scuffle and my father scream out in pain. Running towards the truck, he saw two young men attacking my father. He rushed in to help, but one of the assailants turned and knocked him down. From the ground, he saw the shine of a blade as one of the man repeatedly stabbed my father. My father fell to the ground and Pablo grabbed his body and pulled it under the truck with him. The two men took off running, leaving them both on the ground.

"Pellin, Pellin are you alright?" screamed Pablo as he held my father up against him. He looked down and saw blood gushing out of my father's chest. "Christ, hold on man, hold on. Help, someone help!" he desperately hollered.

"It's no good," gasped *papi que se murio.*

"Shhh, don't talk, just hold on. It's going to be okay," said Pablo.

"Carmin, Carmin…aggh you have to take care of her," groaned my father, closing his eyes. Pablo held him tightly muttering reassurances, but he died in his arms at 12:10 a.m. Carmin, which was one of my mother's nicknames, was the last thought he had as he died from a perforated heart.

Mami was awakened by the knock on her door. Frighten, since no one usually knocked at this late time, she cautiously walked to the door. Her heart sank when she saw police officers accompanied by Pablo at the door. Trembling, she opened the door. Her worst fears were realized. She crumpled to the floor in shock and was rushed to the hospital as well.

The next evening, she sat numbly reading the newspaper, "He could have paid no attention…but he followed his decent instincts," wrote the local paper. "He valiantly gave his life to protect and defend the property of others…Pedro Garcia was the type of man who accepted responsibility, the role of a good citizen, and tried to assist our law enforcement authorities," shared the police chief. He died a hero. He was just 28 years old, at the prime of his life, killed over soda cases.

This was not part of her life plan. At that time, she was living the life that was expected of her. Marriage and family were the ultimate goals and accomplishments, and she had succeeded at this only to have it abruptly stripped away from her. At 24 years old, she found herself widowed with five children. She was overwhelmed by the enormity of this tragic turn of events.

To add to her stress, relatives of the accused terrorized her by throwing rocks through her window. I was sitting on the sofa when the attack ensued and glass and rocks fell on me, leaving me with a scratched cornea and a permanent knob on my skull. She had to move out for her own safety. Fortunately, the two assailants were caught and brought to justice.

The community, moved by my father's heroism and tragic death, mobilized and raised funds for the Pedro Garcia Trust Fund. The Puerto Rican Family Center, the Sokol

Organizations, the Bridgeport Detective Division, the Police Union, and the Benevolent Association all united, transcending nationalities and cultural lines, to raise funds to benefit us.

Mami often shared that one of her greatest laments was that he never got to see Lilly walk. They were already aware that something was developmentally wrong with Lilly. As a couple, they spent a lot of time trying to teach Lilly to walk. They would sit on the floor with her, coaxing her to take a step. Or they would each take a hand and walk her around the room. It was frightening for them not knowing what Lilly would be capable of, yet they were determined to support and help her. It was their first major challenge as a young couple, and Mami was so sad that he didn't get to reap the fruit of his hard labor when Lilly finally mastered her first steps.

His children meant everything to him. At first, he only wanted boys. Purportedly, he had a negative attitude towards women, perceiving them as untrustworthy. Mami would joke that consequently God "cursed" him with four girls to teach him a lesson. She laughed at the irony. His first baby was Evelyn or as we call her, Evi. Evi was a beautiful blonde baby girl with bright blue eyes. Two years later, she was followed by Eric, a big boy with dark blonde hair and hazel eyes, greatly resembling Evi. To their unexpected surprise, nine months later Silvia came along. She was a teeny baby, born two-months early as a preemie. She had the darker hair and eyes of my father. Lilly and I came along two years after.

By this pregnancy, Mami was the one that really wanted another boy. After she had Lilly, she laid exhausted on the bed when the doctor startled her by announcing, "There's another one, push." She was not expecting twins! Four minutes later, I came along. Mami lifted her head and just barely got out, "is it a boy?" Upon discovering that she had yet again another girl, she fainted. Two more teeny babies, with dark blonde hair and brown eyes added to the family.

This young family is captured in a family portrait I keep in an antique frame in my living room. This portrait conjures up images of my father. In it, I sit in the middle with my chubby cheeks and a big puffy bun atop of my head. I remember asking Mami, "What's up with my hair?"

"He combed your hair," Mami proudly replied.

Cute, but I look like a cone head – lucky me! Though I laugh, I cherish the picture. I visualize him taking the time to comb my hair. My father was from the generation where men were the breadwinners and women were the caretakers. Roles were pretty defined and divided, especially among Puerto Rican men. Yet, he took the time to comb both Lilly's and my hair to get us ready for this portrait. I could imagine him struggling with my unruly curls, trying to create a neat, sleek bun. Instead, hair is coming out of the side of my head where he couldn't pull it tight enough to contain it in the bun, and then the bun itself is like a bird's nest sitting on my head. Think of Larry from the *Three Stooges* and add a bun to his head and that's me! Lilly's wasn't much better. Hers doesn't even look like a bun, but rather like a rooster's comb in the front of her head. It's actually funny, and it creates an image of my father patiently and lovingly taking care of his girls.

Besides his children, his passion in life was baseball. He played shortstop in a softball league. When he wasn't playing softball, he played dominoes. He excelled in both areas, winning local and regional trophies. After his death, both baseball and dominoes continued to be a huge part of our life. He also was very health conscious, way before the current health craze. He did weight lifting, he drank homemade protein drinks, he exercised, and he loved dancing. Although he was very popular and beloved, I got the impression that he was private and introverted.

He hated having pictures taken. Growing up none of us ever knew what he looked like. It's hard to describe what it feels like not to know what your father looks like. You're left with only your imagination. We only had one picture of his back where he is showing off his muscles to the camera. He was very toned, had very nicely groomed hair, and looked very attractive.

Mami claimed that he looked like a cross between Silvia and Eric. He had Silvia's thinner and darker hair and her more olive complexion. His mother had a few pictures of him but she refused to show them to us. This was a bone of contention with Mami, and she greatly resented it. It was just explained to us that our grandmother was eccentric and possessive of the pictures.

After he died, we were not close to our paternal side of the family. I have a few recollections of family gatherings playing with my cousins and uncles. But these were rare times. We really never knew why we were not close, but, regardless of the reason, we felt rejected.

I remember a time that Mami dropped us off at my grandmother's house while she ran around to take care of final arrangements for her mother's funeral. My grandmother wasn't very nurturing and didn't really interact with us. We sat in the living room watching television. All of a sudden, my *Tia Tita* came by to check in on us and got into an argument with her mother. She was upset with her mother because she was eating McDonald's food in front of us and had not offered us any food. In reality, we were too upset about *abuela's* death to eat, but it was very sweet of my aunt to come to our defense. She understood our emotional state and lovingly coaxed us into eating. I never saw them again for another twenty years.

In our most petty moments, Silvia and I would verbalize our desire to see them again just so that they could see that we grew up okay, that we graduated college, and formed great families of our own, wanting to flaunt this in their face for rejecting us.

We didn't reconnect with them until I was 32 years old. After bumping into one of my uncles from our maternal side, they called us and extended an invitation to visit. We were all very surprised and curious. We went to the visit a bit apprehensively. I was very pleased to meet a humble, religious and loving family that excitedly welcomed my family. It was obvious that they wanted to make a good impression and make us feel welcomed. Needless to say, there was no flaunting on Silvia's and my part. We don't know why the estrangement existed, and we certainly didn't ask why. We just gratefully reconnected and enjoyed the opportunity to extend our family circle.

It was during this visit that I finally saw two pictures of my father. One picture was on a plaque made in his honor by his baseball league and another was a picture of him with the team. Years of imagining were finally put to rest. At last, there was a face to the stories. Of course, he looked nothing like I expected.

Besides having a little of Silvia's look, his personality was supposed to be just like hers. That is to say that he was supposed to be head-strong. My sister is introverted, independent, and a Vegan who is highly committed to exercise and healthy living. While I am the queen of balance, she is the queen of extremes. I could certainly imagine the similarities between Silvia and him. Like him, she loves dancing, exercising and is definitely private.

Mami said they were inseparable and that she was his "little spy." Apparently, he could be jealous and controlling, not allowing my mother to socialize without him. So Silvia, who was just an innocent toddler, would tell him if my mother looked out the window or spoke to anyone. This would result in huge arguments between them. To add fuel to the fire, Mami's friends and relatives would put it into her head that Silvia was possessed. They even recommended exorcism! She was just a baby who idolized her dad. She probably rejected my mother in favor of him. However, anyone who is a parent knows the feeling of a child favoring one parent. You also know enough not to put any credence in it. But I think that people fed the fire and made Mami unnecessarily insecure.

Because of some of these stories, I confess that at times I did not have the best image of my father. I imagined him to be conservative and *machista* (chauvinistic). We would tease that if he had lived, we would have become nuns. Mami also shared that he once slapped her. "I called the cops and threw his ass in jail, and he never ever did that again," she boasted as she tried to teach me the importance of not tolerating any kind of abuse from a man. Nonetheless, combing my hair for my portrait doesn't seem very *machista*. Consequently, my image of him flipped flopped between a hero and a controlling man – quite an enigma.

Mami always said that God takes the good ones because He needs them as angels. In a final letter to us, she wrote how *papi que se murio* was the only man that ever truly loved her - very poignant words for my mother. Today I give him a place of honor and glory in my memories and prayers. From him I learned the importance of always stepping up and doing the right thing. I admire his courage and convictions. His death forever instilled in me an understanding that life is fragile. This didn't make me fatalistic, but rather it made me appreciative of every day.

I've always embraced the knowledge that I'm going to die and that's okay. I haven't needed a life altering experience to begin to value every moment of my life. Growing up, I lived with the belief that you show your love now, you express your feelings now, you don't waste time holding on to anger and hurt feelings. I've experienced many deaths in my family and seen firsthand the regrets that people hold on to. My father's death gave me this gift, this insight, right from the beginning.

Papi

From left to right: Lilly and me

Lilly

THERE COMES A time when life veers in an unforeseen direction, a turning point that forever impacts you. For me that point was the day my twin sister, Lilly, was institutionalized.

Up to this point, we were living a typical middle class life surrounded by our extended family. My grandmother lived in the apartment below us, and we had our cousins and uncles around us. I was too young at this point to realize that some elements of this environment were like gangrene waiting to spread and infest the healthy organs around it. All I knew was that we had playmates, a yard, a home in a nice neighborhood, and loving grandparents. However, my mother realized the risks and literally amputated them from our life. The opportunity to separate came with the decision to institutionalize Lilly.

Lilly was born four minutes before me. I was the unexpected twin. We were born in a Catholic hospital, and weighing only four pounds apiece, they needed to baptize us as a precaution in case one of us didn't survive, so I had to be quickly named. Thus, I ended up with my mother's name, Elizabeth.

By all accounts, Lilly appeared healthy. She was a beautiful baby girl, in fact, the prettier twin. Her features were more refined than mine, and her head full of soft curls. I had the round face, big forehead, and frizzy curls. I started walking as most children did a little after my first birthday. However, Lilly was yet to take her first steps. My toddler vocabulary grew in English and Spanish, but Lilly was still silent, uttering only random sounds.

My parents knew that something wasn't right, and the doctors confirmed it. I don't know the actual diagnosis, but in those days it was simply known as severe "mental retardation." At seven years old, Lilly was still unable to communicate, to use the bathroom consistently, or to function independently.

Despite her limitations, she was my companion, always by my side. I may not have been able to express myself to her, but I still shared this connectedness with her. We walked hand in hand. We played side by side. We bathed together and slept together. It was a natural reflex for me to reach out to feed her or help her with the simplest tasks.

Sitting in the living room watching television, I could hear the persistent sibilant humming of the tin spinning top as Lilly pushed the auger up and down. At Lilly's guttural noises, I glanced her way and saw her contently staring at the top. Switching my attention back to the television, I engrossed myself back to my show.

Moments later I heard, "Bonk, Bonk, Bonk." Quickly I looked towards Lilly who was now rhythmically banging her head against the wall. I jumped off the sofa and ran to her. I grabbed her shoulder and tried to pull her away from the wall.

"Uggh," she grunted in anger at my futile attempts to stop her and continued to bang her head undisturbed.

"Mami!" I called for help. Lilly was stronger than me, and I couldn't get her to stop. Together we pulled Lilly away from the wall. Angry at us for interrupting her, she grabbed my sweater. Howling like a howler monkey, she held me in her tight grip. Mami began to pry her fingers, trying to release her fist. Lilly screamed louder and stubbornly held on. Together we began to loosen her grip, but Lilly quickly changed strategy and grabbed Mami's hair instead. Mami's head was now twisted down as Lilly pulled her hair. I again tried to release Lilly's fist. After what felt like an eternity but was probably five minutes, Lilly released her, got up, and walked away as if nothing happened. These episodes were routine for Lilly. Head banging, with its rhythmic movement just like the top's movement, was comforting for her but frightening for us. Grabbing people by the hair or shirt occurred unexpectedly and repeatedly, sometimes in direct response to frustration, but other times the attack appeared not to be prompted by anything.

Lilly lived in her own world, and it was hard to know how aware she was of her environment. One summer afternoon we were all playing outside while Lilly sat in the porch with her spinning top. One of the neighbor's children began to get into an argument with us. Out of nowhere, Lilly came rushing towards us waving a stick to hit the boy.

Frightened, he took off running as Lilly gave chase. Taken aback by her attempt to defend us, we quickly ran after her to prevent her from attacking the boy.

Because of her special needs, my mother imposed little discipline on her. Mami did not feel comfortable pushing her to learn basic skills. Mami washed her teeth, bathed her, fed her, and took her to the bathroom. Mami didn't have the firm hand needed to help my sister learn and developmentally grow, and the community did not have the support system to help families with children with special needs. Thus, Lilly was making little progress gaining basic skills.

One day my younger sister, Rose, who was just a toddler, was standing by the flight of stairs. Suddenly Lilly dashed at her and shoved her down the stairs. "No!" screamed Mami as she rushed down the stairs to Rose.

"Oh my God is she okay?"

Frantically, Mami checked Rose and comforted her. She sat at the base of the stairs cradling Rose and crying along with her. "I can't do this anymore," she repeatedly said as she rocked Rose back and forth.

For years Lilly's doctor had been advising Mami to institutionalize Lilly. This incident came in the heels of Lilly yanking an earring off of Evi's ear, ripping her earlobe. In the 60's, institutionalization was the norm for the treatment of people with disabilities. Mami had resisted for seven years. In defeat, she called the doctor and made the decision to place Lilly in Mansfield Training School. I can only imagine the pain this decision caused my mother and certainly the confusion it caused my sister, who for the rest of her life suffered from separation anxiety. As for me, a part of my life was ripped away.

The drive to Mansfield, Connecticut was gloomy. A piercing silence enveloped the car, casting each of us into our own melancholy reverie. I hung my hand out the window, feeling the wind pushing and raising my hand. Engrossed in my fantasy of escape, I was a bird soaring freely, swooping up and down, enjoying the landscape below.

We finally arrived to this picturesque rural town. Mansfield was originally settled by farmers, and it remains a rural town today. It was quite different than the inner city where we lived. Mansfield was sparsely populated. It has beautiful rolling hills, with tree-lined roads that created a green canvas right before my eyes. Streams and ponds could be seen between the trees. The roads curved and the single family homes were separated by acres of land. The whiff of cows from the dairy farms permeated the air. Silence was everywhere. It definitely was not like our neighborhood where two and three family houses were in close proximity, and children played up and down the streets. We entered another world.

A heavy tension surrounded us as we approached Mansfield Training School. The school sat on 1,000 acres of land and was comprised of 85 buildings. Some of the buildings were large, brick institutional looking buildings, in sharp contrast to the historic town that it resided in. We walked into a large brick building. Immediately a strong, palpable odor greeted us. It was so acrid that I had to breathe through my mouth. The odor was the smell of the cleaning products used, not the lemony fresh smell that you would use in your house, but the strong commercial antiseptic smell that I will forever associate with Mansfield Training School.

I held on to my brother's hand in fear as we walked down the corridor. The hallway was long with bare cream walls that also had portions of glassed in walls interspersed through the corridor. We walked in a tight group, shoulder to shoulder, afraid to even stray one inch from each other. As I passed the window sections, I saw patients sitting around. Some were drooling; others sat in wheel chairs bent in awkward positions, while others walked around screaming or laughing to themselves. My senses were overwhelmed with unfamiliar smells, noises, and sights. Some of the more curious patients approached us – looking to touch, hug, and talk to us, but instead instilling a tremendous fear in me.

A tall girl came up to me. "Hello," she said as she gave me a big hug. Remembering how Lilly loved to pull my hair, I flinched uneasily fearing that the friendly hug would turn violent. A knot grew tight in my stomach, making it hard for me to breathe. I could feel the tears wanting to come out, burning behind my eyelids trying to escape. Gulping and pasting a forced smile, I stood still doing everything I could to hold them in. Just as I was feeling overwhelmed by the unfamiliarity of this new environment, Lilly, too, sensed that something was out of the ordinary. Reacting quickly, she jumped into my mother's arms, winding her strong legs around her waist and her arms around her neck.

I stared at Lilly and felt my throat constrict. Oh God, I can't breathe!

A worker tried to take Lilly, who started screaming and crying. My mother stood there totally helpless. She was now crying, trying to talk Lilly down. More workers came to help peel Lilly off. We huddled together not knowing what to do, staring at this scene – feeling totally helpless and frightened. It took three staff members to get Lilly off of Mami. They carried her away, screaming and crying. I didn't even get a chance to say good-bye. She was torn from my life as well, leaving me utterly dejected.

This image burns in my mind. The smells and noises are still so real, so present. Tears escape my eyes every time I remember. It is unanimously the worst memory that my siblings and I share – a memory forever imprinted on our collective hearts.

I'm convinced that this was the point that forever changed my mother. Now that I'm a mother, I cannot imagine her horror and pain. I still cry because she went through this agonizing experience. She never forgave herself for this decision. It destroyed her emotionally. She was 29 years old and up to this point she never had taken a drink. All I know is that our life completely changed right after this move.

I continued to feel my connection to Lilly. I would be laughing and all of a sudden I would hear her laughing. My mind would soar to her side, and I would see her laughing just like me. It felt as if we both were laughing at the same time across the distance that separated us.

I cannot describe how I felt. As a twin, I had a lot of unanswered questions. Why did Lilly have to go through this, and why did I come out healthy and she didn't? It was terribly unfair, and I felt guilty. I could have been the one in her shoes. One minute she was home with her brother and sisters and the next she was living amongst strangers. A feeling of insecurity and vulnerability took residence in my heart, consuming me with unsettling, conflicting emotions that raged through me.

Often I had a recurring dream. In this dream, I would be talking and laughing with Lilly, in awe that I could communicate with her.

"Oh my God, how are you? How do you feel? Do you like chocolate?" I would bombard her with questions trying to know everything about her, grabbing every precious second to bond with her. We would engage in an incredulous conversation filling both of us with laughter and joy.

Then I would awaken to the harsh reality that she wasn't there, and the joy would turn to disillusion that I could never speak to her about her simple likes and dislikes. I yearned to be able to have a conversation with her.

When we visited her, we encountered verbal residents who were much more advanced than Lilly, and I found myself resentful, wishing that Lilly had Downe Syndrome instead or that she could be autistic – any other diagnosis that would allow me to communicate with her or have her back at home. Little did I know that in the future I would be blessed with Priscilla, Frank's second-cousin, whom I consider my niece. Priscilla, who has Downe Syndrome, is my pride and joy.

On most visits, I worried for Lilly's safety. When we would go visit her, I would catch myself searching for any signs of bruises or evidence of mistreatment. I couldn't help being suspicious and thinking the worst. I wish I didn't, but anxiety made me eternally vigilant.

During our visits, we walked the grounds of Mansfield together and played in their playground. We brought her presents and watched her open them. All she really wanted, however, were cookies and sweets. Once she ate one, she persistently begged for another and another as we laughed at her insatiable appetite. But then when the time came to say our good-byes, the crying scene replayed itself as she leaped into Mami's arms. Each wail ripped through me, leaving a trail of helplessness in its wake.

At 18 years old, I assumed guardianship of Lilly and my feelings of responsibility grew. As her guardian, I had to approve all medical or major life decisions. Many of these decisions were excruciating. For instance, due to Lilly's head banging, she suffered from a detached retina. For each examination, subsequent treatment, or surgery, she had to be tranquilized and/or sedated for a couple of days to keep her immobile. The process was unbearable for Lilly who kept trying to pull on the bandages, and it was distress for me who suffered her pain alongside her. After three such treatments, I had to decide whether to continue to approve yet another surgery or allow her to go partially blind. Making this life altering decision weighed incredibly on my conscious. I decided to stop the surgeries in order to spare her ongoing trauma and prayed fervently that each decision was a right one.

After the state of Connecticut faced multiple lawsuits, the announcement came that Mansfield Training School was closing. "The Mansfield Training School is closed: the swamp has finally been drained," said the former Director of the School. With that announcement, I faced the decision of selecting a private provider and group home for her. I was fortunate to find a cozy group home with only three residents. The staff was very warm and professional, and she was in good hands so when years later I relocated to Miami, I decided to leave her there, another decision!

Then ultimately came the most difficult decision of all - whether I should approve a "Do Not Resuscitate" order and let her pass away. This was one final decision that I just could not make!

I received the call one evening while I attended a meeting to prepare for an Emmaus women's retreat. Lilly, who was 44 years old, had fallen. Apparently, she had undiagnosed pancreatitis. Over the phone, the doctor sought my permission to disconnect her. Dispassionately, he rationalized that she did not have much of a life anyway, actually referring to her as a vegetable.

"She's not a vegetable," I defensively countered.

"Sorry, I must've been misinformed," he quickly apologized realizing he overstepped his bounds.

"Look, I'll take a flight out today but don't do anything until I get there," I informed him.

I immediately flew back to Connecticut, and rushed to the hospital where I found her unconscious and hooked to machines. She looked so fragile. The doctor explained her life chances and again brought up the issue of removing all life support equipment.

I couldn't decide. I refused to decide. I told my siblings, "You decide. I'll support your decision, but I cannot do this."

They decided that disconnecting her was for the best. However, Evi and Eric could not bear to be in the room so they stepped out. Silvia stayed with me and stood at the foot of the bed. I sat on the bed and held Lilly's small hand. Gingerly I stroked her hair and face as the doctor explained to us what to expect. He said her heart would just naturally give out without the machine helping her to breathe but that it may take hours. We arranged to have a priest come to give Lilly her last rites and blessings. As an innocent child of God who never knew sin, we just wanted her blessed, but he didn't make it on time.

The doctor disconnected her as I held Lilly's hand. Immediately, Lilly instinctively reached out and grasped my shirt pulling me to her side like she had been doing for a lifetime. The doctor was barely gone from the room, when she immediately passed away with a last grip of my shirt.

She had pulled me so close, that my face rested on her face and a deep sorrow poured out of me. I laid my head on her chest and cried, oblivious to everything around me. The sobs shook my whole body. A part of me was gone. I was inconsolable. Me – the stoic one in the family, the caretaker, the one who had valiantly survived numerous deaths with barely a tear, for the first time ever, just gave in to such an incredible loss.

Thank God for my sisters and brother. They put aside their own pain to be there for me, attending to every detail. I'll be forever grateful to them. Then in an outpouring of love, all my family from my husband's side came to be by my side as well. We had lost my mother-in-law just three months ago and their display of unity and support for me was the greatest gift they could give me.

My precious sister was gone. I prayed that she was in peace, reunited with Mami and *papi que se murio.*

From left to right: Silvia, Eric, Evi, Rose, Lilly, and me before Lilly was institutionalized.

Good-bye Butterflies

A TURTLE SEEMS so innocuous and unremarkable. It's slow, hard, and certainly not a cuddly pet. Yet, if I could choose any animal to describe myself as, it would be a turtle. Turtles date back to 215 million years, making it one of the oldest reptiles and, in my eyes, the ultimate survivor. The turtle carries its house on its back. Home is with him at all times. For five years after we institutionalized Lilly, that's how I felt. We were on the move.

To be closer to Lilly, to move away from the stress of her family in Bridgeport, and to follow Polito, Mami's boyfriend, Mami walked away from her house in Bridgeport and moved to Hartford. The move to Hartford brought many changes to our lives. We went from relative comfort to living in abject poverty. When my father died, my mother was left with funds from a community collection in honor of my father; plus, she also received his insurance money. Unfortunately, managing money was not my mother's forte.

My mother only had an eighth grade education. She went from having a husband who took care of everything to all of a sudden being the head of the household at 24 years old. Four years after my father died, she began to live with another man. They moved to Puerto Rico where she bought a single family house and had my younger sister, Rose. We lived in Bayamon, the second largest city in the island. I don't remember much about Puerto Rico. However, I do remember sitting on the curb with Lilly waiting for my brother and sisters to come home from school. I would put Popsicle sticks in the water that drained into the gutter pretending it was a boat until I could see my siblings coming home, and then I'd rush to greet them.

I also remember an overnight visit to Mami's godmother, who lived in the countryside. The poverty in the country was different than in the United States. Here the houses stood on stilts and were more like huts. They were in such close proximity that you were able to reach across the window to the next hut for a cup of sugar. The drinking glasses were not glass at all, rather they were tin cups. The greatest difference was that there was no indoor plumbing, so we had to use *la letrina*, an outdoor latrine in a wood shed. Using the latrine during the day was a new adventure to embrace. In the evening, it was no longer a fun adventure; instead, it was a scary prospect.

Evening came and I lay in bed with my brother and sisters. The window was open, and I could feel the balmy night air blowing into the room. It was really dark and the noises of the *coquis* (a small frog indigenous to Puerto Rico) created an evening orchestra of natural sounds: "Co-Qui, Co-

Qui." Amidst the *coquis'* lullaby, I could hear the hum of adult conversation.

As I tossed and turned, I felt the urge to go to the bathroom. If I got up and told Mami I had to go to the bathroom, she'll make me go to the *letrina*. It was such a small enclosure with its wood walls. There wasn't even a light or a commode. I don't want to go out there; I could hold it. So I continued to toss in discomfort. As the urge grew, I remember my friend Edwin from Bridgeport telling us his scary stories about the devil and how his black hand would squirm up from hell right through the hole of a latrine and pull an unsuspecting child straight down to hell with him. I was petrified!

I couldn't go out there. To make matters worse, I realized that not only did I have to urinate, but I also had to go number two! Too frightened to go outside and unable to hold it any longer, I did it on the bed. I was mortified and started crying. It was so humiliating. I felt like a baby.

My next clearest memories were of celebrating my first and only *Dia de los Reyes* (Three Kings Day – January 6) in Puerto Rico. Christmas in Puerto Rico is an extended holiday starting in early December and ending on January 25th. After The Three Kings Day, there are three days of observance for each of the wise men. This is then followed by the *Octavas*, eight religious days to glorify the kings and Jesus Christ then the *Octavitas*, eight more days of adoration.

The highlight of the Christmas celebration is Three Kings Day (Epiphany). This day celebrates the arrival of the

Three Wise Men, bearing gifts for baby Jesus. The tradition is to collect grass and place it in a shoe box underneath the bed for the camels to eat. Then the Three Kings would leave presents for the children. Well, we were all so excited to celebrate our first *Dia De Los Reyes* that in place of a shoe box, we collected brown grocery bags and filled them with grass. After all, those camels were going to be really hungry, we surmised. I was ecstatic with this island tradition and for years Mami laughed at what a challenge it was for her to inconspicuously discard the grass.

Before we could adjust to Puerto Rico, Mami decided to leave Rose's father and return to Bridgeport. He was unfaithful and even to the best of my knowledge, he still maintains two separate households, with two wives and two sets of children. Needless to say, Mami did not want any part of that "big happy family." For the cost of airplane tickets, she sold the house to her cleaning woman and returned to America.

Once back in Bridgeport, she bought a three family house in a nice working class neighborhood. We had a front porch and a comfortable backyard with a swing set and a swimming pool. Our yard had fruit trees and sunflowers, which I actually found creepy as they looked like a big eye to me. There were lots of butterflies in our yard. Of course Eric, ever the mischief, made me believe that they would attack me so I hid behind the porch door afraid to go to the yard.

Afterwards we had such great times in that yard. Evi, Silvia, and Eric loved to dive into the pool, jump from the roof, and swing as high as they could from the swing set. I couldn't keep up with them, but I loved their daredevil ways. They always got into trouble, and when Mami disciplined them, they'd pretend to cry, only to start right up again the minute she walked out.

The house also had an attic and a basement. The basement was a major source of entertainment. I would pretend to be a witch, and the basement was my domain. When I was not playing in it pretending it was my witch's lair, my *abuelo* (grandfather) used it as a makeshift movie studio. *Abuelo* would film 8mm horror movies in the basement. As one of the younger children, my roles would be silent parts – a mummy, a zombie, a dead body. We had so much fun making these movies and waiting for the next inspiration to strike my *Abuelo*.

I also loved playing in the house, sliding down the banister and using pillows to slide down the stairs. We would all go walking around the neighborhood, which included a mad dash by the cemetery, followed by our highlight, a stop at the laundry mat. We were all small skinny children and easily fit inside the big dryers. We would take turns getting inside, while Evi or Eric would spin us around. We laughed and laughed as we were tumbled in our personalized amusement ride.

Although this time was idyllic for us, it was difficult for Mami. Instead of renting the two apartments for income, her brother occupied one apartment and her mother another – both rent free. My mother never worked, and things quickly became unbearable for her.

It was around this time that Mami decided to institutionalize Lilly and moved us all to Hartford. We faced another move, but this time we were leaving our family, our friends, our school – our home. Teary eye and frightened by the unknown, I left everything that represented security to me. And once again, she simply gave away her house to her mother and walked away. We went from a working class environment straight to a ghetto.

We lived in such destitute environments that even if I wanted my children to see where I grew up, there is nothing for me to show them. Every apartment that we ever lived in was condemned and demolished.

Our first move was to Walnut Street where we lived across a highway ramp in a brick apartment building that housed six families. Another similar building was adjacent to our building. The street then went up a small hill with no other property along it. We lived in the outskirts of downtown Hartford, so it really wasn't a residential area. The apartment buildings had three floors with two apartment units on each floor.

Each floor had a back porch that overlooked a yard that was approximately 25 by 40 feet wide. Unlike our house in Bridgeport, this yard didn't have trees, bushes, swimming pool or swings. The backyard view was of rows of garbage cans across the yard on top of a cement block. In place of butterflies, we now had rats. The sunflowers that looked like big eyes were replaced with the real eyes of rats. These rats became our source of entertainment.

"Look, there," Eric pointed at a thick brown tail scurrying behind a trash can. Patiently, we all took position with our rocks and with bated breath waited for the next sighting. Plop, plop, plop…we hurled our rocks at the rat in our version of "hit the can."

Because rats also made their way into the apartment along with the cockroaches, Mami would put rat poison around the apartment and porch. One day we were all in the kitchen hanging out when Rose ran in screaming. Her hand was outstretched and hanging from the webbing between her thumb and her pointer was a wiggly huge, brown rat. We all screamed in shock as Mami moved fast to remove the rodent. The rat didn't release Rose quickly, and Mami had to swipe and pull on it. It fell on the floor and lay there all woozy. It had eaten some of the poison and that's what made it possible for Rose to approach it and attempt to pet it, thinking it was a cat curled in the corner. She had to be rushed to the hospital.

In addition to rodents, the apartment was around the corner to a homeless community, filled with drug addicts, prostitutes, and alcoholics. We had to pass through this street to get to the local *bodega* (corner store), the church, and the school. One day Eric came home from school terribly ill. He was feverish, nauseous and weak. He complained of body aches. Somehow Eric contracted Hepatitis B and soon we all broke out as well. Oh, what miserable days! Eric had it the worst. He became jaundiced and terribly weak. We all got feverish and nauseous. As part of the treatment, we had to undergo frequent blood work. Nothing could be worse for me. I was petrified of needles and now it seemed like I was getting poked every day. What a nightmare!

Besides throwing rocks at rats, our other favorite pastime was sliding down a small hill, more of a mound, which separated the highway ramp with our street. We would roll down this mound as if it was a green giant rolling hill. We would also ride our bike down this mound. We had one bicycle for five children so we were very creative in piling onto the bike. One person peddled, usually Eric or Evi, another sat on the steering wheel (usually Silvia or me), and one stood on the back. Fearlessly, we rode up and down our street.

These were the late 60s, a turbulent time in many inner cities across the nation. Mami was active in the civil rights movement.

"If you don't vote, then don't complain," she would tell us.

Glued to the television, she kept apprised of the latest activities.

"Come, *nenas*, we're going to a rally."

Excitedly, we loaded onto a bus and enjoyed a bus ride filled with singing. At the church, I joined the children in play as the adults met and organized. Evening came, and we slept on the floor. The room was filled with great music and a sense of camaraderie filled the room. While the adults attended the rally, we stayed at the church playing, oblivious to the political turmoil around us.

Hartford, like other urban cities, was torn by race riots. Few people associate Connecticut with urban strife and challenges; instead, they visualize Hartford as a quaint wealthy town. The reality is that although Connecticut is a wealthy state, it also has huge gaps in income between the residents of the inner cities and the suburban towns. Racial tension existed just as it did throughout most metropolitan areas. Serious outbreaks occurred in the north end of Hartford where we lived. Violence peaked on Labor Day 1969 when mobs of people battled with police, set fire to a public library, and damaged almost one hundred buildings. Over 500 people were arrested.

Because of our proximity to the highway, many white professionals from downtown drove by our apartment building and into a barrage of rocks flung to their cars. The children collected rocks and piled them up for the adults to use. The street felt electrified by all the commotion.

I felt a combination of excitement and fear by the confusing events unfolding before me. This feeling was replaced with horror when an older woman, probably in her late 60s, had the misfortune of driving into our neighborhood. The rocks started flying, but this time a man came out of nowhere, ran to the car, opened her door and grabbed at the woman to get her purse. The woman cried furiously, scared and powerless. Some of the adults were outraged at this man and chased the thief away, but the unfortunate woman was left shaken and robbed.

Soon I heard the blasting police sirens. "Run, run get inside," Mami urged as she shepherded us into our first floor apartment. Everyone ran back into the apartments like a stampede of horses behind us. Through the open curtain, I could see the bright red and blue police strobe lights.

"Get away from there," Mami said pulling the curtains. The noise around me increased between the pounding of footsteps running up the stairs to the apartment above and the police officer speaking on his bullhorn outside. All of a sudden, a loud crash resounded over my head. I ducked as the window shattered and a projectile landed right in our living room and directly onto Evi's ankle. Confused and frighten, I stared at the foreign object that spurted out a gas. My eyes started to sting and I screamed, alarmed.

"Get to the floor," yelled Mami. I dived to the floor where my brother and sisters were huddled. Now I was petrified. My eyes were hurting and tears were streaming down my face, both from the gas and from fear. Evi was howling, screeching "It burns, it burns!" At first I thought her eyes were hurting like mine were. I closed my eyes harder and rubbed at them trying to get rid of the stinging. Mami ran to Evi and noticed that she had been burned on her ankle. Luis, Mami's boyfriend, rushed into the living room and shoved a wet towel in my hand, "cover your eyes," he instructed and moved similarly to the others.

I grabbed the towel and lay prone on the floor. My heart was pounding. Because I couldn't clearly see what was happening around me and with Evi, much less understand it, everything felt like a living nightmare that was worse than any bogey-man I could have conjured.

With a loud crashing noise, I heard the police busting in through the door, screaming commands. Evi, with Mami by her side, was rushed to the hospital with a second degree burn on her ankle.

Alas, the building was condemned, and we moved to another rotten neighborhood where rats and cockroaches continued to abound instead of the colorful and delicate butterflies we had left behind.

Me at age 9

Proud to Be A Coward

EVENTUALLY OUR FAMILY moved to Charter Oak Terrace, a low-income housing project, when I was nine years old. I was apprehensive as we pulled into the projects. The housing units were compacted together, and looked so drab with their uniform look.

"I really don't want to be here," I sullenly whined to Eric.

"I know, it's ugly," he concurred.

"Come on," Mami piped in. "It's going to be great," she cheerily announced. After three moves in three years time, I was quite skeptical. The idea of starting at a new school and making new friends was very distressing. I just wanted to wallow in my bad mood.

"Here we are!"

Our apartment was in the corner. The building was a long unit with six, side-by-side two-story apartments.

"At least we don't have to share hallways with others," I noted.

I liked that our apartment was on the far end so we were not sandwiched between two tenants. We also were on the outside street where the project ended. So the front of our unit faced a church, a warehouse, and a corner store (Shorty's) - prime location. We entered from the back entrance, where the parking area was. As we walked in, we faced an alcove that led down to a crawl space that connected all the units. To my immediate left was a small kitchen. On the wall to the right was the stove and sink with overhead cabinets. Along the width of the western wall was the refrigerator. There was a steam radiator and a window overlooking the yard on the eastern wall. The northern wall was the outside wall that had another window in the kitchen and led to the base of a stairway that separated the kitchen from a good size square living room. Eric bounded up the stairs to get first dibs among the bedrooms.

"Not fair!" Silvia and I shouted scrambling behind him.

At the top of the stairs, two bedrooms were to the left and the master bedroom and bathroom to the right. Eric grabbed the first bedroom which had a flat roof in the outside of the window, leaving us with the corner room.

"What do you mean I have to share with Rose?" Eric argued with Mami as Silvia and I rushed to our room snickering at him.

After so many moves, I figured this will be just another pit stop; however, I lived in this project right up to the day Mami died when I was 18 years old.

How can I fairly describe Charter Oak Terrace? With great difficulty! Let me start with basic, unemotional facts. Charter Oak Terrace was originally built as a 1,000 unit development for military families during World War II. It was inhabited by mostly white families but then became home primarily to low-income Puerto Rican families. The housing project deteriorated to an ill-maintained, highly-dense, neglected community rampant with gang violence, drugs, and crime. It was demolished in the late 1990's amidst controversy about the displacement of low-income families who called Charter Oak Terrace home.

Now here's the emotional description of Charter Oak Terrace. First, it was a trap for cycle after cycle of intergenerational poverty. Grandmother, mother, and daughter would all end up there raising their single family household. Like quicksand, once you were sucked in, there was no getting out. It created a comfortable, familiar neighborhood that was home for so many families. So even though it was cockroach infested and crime infected – it was home. I know that Mami would never have moved out had she lived; Evi was there until it was finally demolished. Ironically, it represented security for too many people, a familiar environment less threatening than the larger society outside. To me it was a stifling cage that I longed to leave behind.

Although Mami kept an orderly and clean house, it had a terrible roach infestation. It is so true: nothing kills cockroaches – I completely believe the rumors that they will survive a nuclear explosion. Mami would spray, use fumigating bombs, call for professional fumigating services, and the cockroaches would just run next door and come back with a vengeance. They were everywhere. Simply sitting on the sofa relaxing was interrupted with a warning scream, "behind you!" I would jump off the sofa just in time to miss the flying shoe that Eric shot across with deadly accuracy.

At bath time, the tub required a thorough rinsing first. Similarly, every dish, cup, utensil had to be thoroughly rinsed before each use. The worst part, or if you were a crazy boy like Eric, the most exciting part, was turning on the light at night to surprise hundreds of little brown roaches scrambling away. To Eric this was the ultimate challenge, a call to battle in a war that he could never win. For me, it wasn't a battle at all, but rather a hamster wheel where no matter how hard I ran, I would get nowhere! With disgust I had to check my shoes and my books every morning to avoid inadvertently carrying a roach to school, which unfortunately occurred a couple of times. The most terrible part was right after we fumigated. The cockroaches would drop straight from the ceiling, like rain drops, leaving a carpet of dead roaches on the floor for us to clean up.

The apartment had a tiny yard probably 20 by 20 feet. A clothesline extended across the length of the yard to a metal pole. One day someone was throwing out a rose bush. Excitedly, I asked if I could have it and eagerly planted it in my little yard. It looked lonely next to the metal pole so I decided to plant some marigolds and zinnias. They grew nice and tall. It was not a manicured garden with mulch or anything, but it added some color to the otherwise drab environment.

The worst part of Charter Oak Terrace was that it was rife with violence. Just walking to school was an adventure. Silvia and Eric were in middle school and Rose attended a special school for the deaf, so I had to walk alone to my elementary school. It wasn't a bad school, and I liked my teacher. But walking home was another story. I was afraid of the residents from the adjacent project, Rice Heights.

My neighbors, Carmen and her two sisters, attended the same school as me so we walked together.

"Remember, always walk quickly through this section," they advised me.

"Why?" I asked.

"You'll see," they said with a smile.

As we approached the light, a group of older kids were coming down from Rice Heights. Once they saw us, they quickly gave chase.

"Run!" Carmen screamed as I took off following.

The group laughed as they turned towards their bus stop.

"They're so stupid," Carmen said.

The Rice Heights residents did not mix with Charter Oak residents; hence, they periodically chased or harassed us as we passed the outskirts of their project.

I noticed that we would take the long way to school instead of cutting through the projects, sticking to the outside streets.

"You don't want to take that short cut," Carmen explained. "There may be fights; it's best to take the long way."

Taking me under her wings, Carmen taught me how to safely navigate Charter Oak, which essentially meant sitting on our back stoop, watching life around us.

Charter Oak Terrace was the breeding ground for the Savage Nomads, a 70's gang. In the 70s, stabbings were more popular than the current drive-by shootings. It was not uncommon for us to be sitting on the stoop, when a car would drive fast by us and block the exit. Looking up, we could see a car blocking the other side. Men jumped out of the cars and attacked their victim using bats, carjacks, and/or knives. As quickly as it started, they would jump back in their cars, leaving the person barely alive. At least twice, two men did not survive the attack, murdered right before my eyes.

When these scenes played themselves out, I was always amazed by the number of people who brazenly ran to get a front row view. You would think you were visiting a circus, with an electrified audience in awe of the performance in front of them, laughing and talking about the parties involved and what had led up to the fight as if they were not actually witnessing someone getting beaten to a pulp. Many seemed oblivious to the danger, because sure enough the frenetic crowd led to angry words, a shove, and another brawl would ensue. I detested being near this pool of piranhas who fed off the violence and drama; instead I would make a mad dash into my house. I was and am a proud coward.

Shame

MAMI WAS VERY protective. As a single mother, she felt she had to be extra strict, serving as both mother and father. She felt she failed with Evi who ran-away from home soon after we arrived to Bridgeport. Over-compensating, we were not allowed to wander beyond our unit, usually not beyond the stoop outside of our door.

I associated with exactly two families – both at the end of our building. Everyone was treated suspiciously, as someone who could hurt, corrupt, or get me ensnared in a life style I didn't want to be in. Besides the fear of violence, a very real threat of getting trapped there existed. For any young woman, that meant pregnancy – the quickest way to guarantee a future in the projects. Needless to say, Mami kept us on a very short-leash.

I'm quite ashamed to admit that I was embarrassed to live in Charter Oak. Worse, there were times when I was embarrassed to be Puerto Rican. No child should ever be ashamed of their heritage, and I'm sorry that I ever was, especially as I should have known better.

Mami pushed two primary values: *Orgullo* (pride) and *Respeto* (respect). One of these two words would invariably slip her lips as she disciplined and parented us. *Respeto* was respect for others, especially your elders. There was a way to speak, look, and act before others. Every adult family member was greeted with a hug, kiss, and "*pidiendo la bendicion*," asking to be blessed. If you failed to give the proper greeting, you were reprimanded. We had to give up our seats for the adults and not interrupt adult conversations. We also never challenged an adult. Any contrary opinion or perspective we had from an adult was expressed privately among ourselves with Mami.

Respeto also extended to how we treated her and each other. Typical sibling fighting was rare in our house. Confrontations were avoided. If you were upset, you simply wrote a letter. Mami left witty notes on the bathroom sink saying, "please wash me, wash me" or on the floor, "sweep me please, I have allergies." These funny notes were strategically placed as needed around the house in lieu of a lecture. If we didn't find a note, we would come home from school to find that all of our clothes drawers were emptied on the floor. It was time to clean your drawers and that was that. We rarely raised our voices against each other, much less hit one another. One look from Mami, accompanied by her famous raising of one warning hand, quickly quelled any squabbling.

Orgullo or pride was not being proud in the sense of being vain or boastful, but in taking pride in yourself, your family, your nationality, your country. We knew all about our island of Puerto Rico – its geography, its history and its culture. We spoke Spanish to the point that my daughter teases me about my accent, not understanding how I could have one since I was born in America. *Orgullo* meant patriotism and loyalty to the United States, to the history of collaboration between the two nations. It meant having pride in being a citizen of both countries. *Orgullo* covered how you carried yourself. For instance, when we ate in people's house, we were to always leave a little food on the plate. To Mami this indicated that we were not poor or starving.

A *faux pas* in social manners made you look like a *"jibara."* For a Puerto Rican, a *jibaro*, a word for someone from the country, carries two meanings. The good and popular meaning is the representation of a traditional humble, hard working, simple Puerto Rican with good solid values. On the flip side, it also means an uneducated, ignorant person, who is easily fooled and misled. If you dressed inappropriately, you were a *jibara*. If you didn't have social graces, you were a *jibara*. If you couldn't speak up and articulate intelligently, you were a *jibara*.

"Deja de ser tan jibara" (stop being such a *jibara*) prompted us to step up, and take a risk.

Orgullo embodied all these values. It seemed to fit all disciplinary scenarios.

"Mira muchacha, orgullo," (Pride, little girl) quickly put us in our place.

This concept of the *jibaro* is affectionately captured in the celebrated folk character, *Juan Bobo* (Foolish John). Children and adults alike eagerly looked forward to the adventures, or rather misadventures, of *Juan Bobo*, who always managed to blunder through his greatest intentions. Mami affectionately passed down these folklores and traditions to ensure that we grew up with solid Puerto Rican values and pride.

But parents alone do not raise their children. We were surrounded, unfortunately, in an environment where too many adults were not positive role models. Thus, it was easy to equate the poor, inner-city culture with being a Puerto Rican. Too many people proudly linked being Puerto Rican with being tough, low-income, uneducated, violent, or simply a criminal. Of course, this fallacy can't be furthest from the truth. We are as diverse as any other culture, with great scholars, artists, leaders, and families and with our share of criminals, addicts, and dysfunctional families. In Charter Oak, there were many decent families who shared their limited resources and worked hard to provide for their families. Regrettably, the bad apples had a way of shining and overshadowing all the others. Furthermore, the Puerto Ricans that did make it out of poverty became obscured in the suburban landscape.

The stereotypes about Puerto Ricans were reinforced by both the white community and our own people and were internalized. When white people resorted to the stereotypes, they were accused of being a racist. But when a Puerto Rican mocked you as trying to be white if you were smart, had plans to go to college, or aspired for anything beyond the projects, that was acceptable. Few understood what an awful insult to your own culture those taunts were! How tragic and damaging.

As a result, in school I was very private. I kept to myself and revealed little about me. As a fair-skin Puerto Rican, I fit in both cultures and very easily could make myself invisible and unnoticeable. I was a good student, studious, generally quiet and involved in school activities. Although I was active in school, I feared rejection from both the white and the Puerto Rican community. Isolation was the result. My only true friend was my mother and Carmen.

My greatest shame came the day of my Future Business Leaders of America (FBLA) competition. I'm not very competitive; hence, I was anxious but excited in my first competitive experience. I was the school representative for the stenography competition, where I went on to win first place. Our team did really well, and we were all pumped and excited.

"I'm so proud of all of you," beamed Mrs. Levine.

"I've never gotten 107 words a minute," I shared.

"Me, too, I can't believe I typed 65 words a minute. My fingers were cramping!"

Giggling, we basked in recounting our accomplishments.

"Elizabeth, I think you're the closest. Where do I drop you off?" asked Mrs. Levine.

My heart stopped as my excitement at having won the stenography competition quickly dissipated, replaced with great apprehension.

"I'll give you directions," I told her. I looked at the beautiful neighborhood in West Hartford, a suburban town across the tracks from where I lived and became self conscious. Here the neighborhood consisted of all private homes with shutters, hedges, and manicured lawns. There were no clothes hanging on clotheslines, no toys in the front yard, no broken down cars randomly abandoned.

"What do I do?" I pondered, mad at myself for presuming to participate in the competition. Because of my stupid ego, I was facing this dilemma.

No one knew anything about me and now I was in a car filled with white, middle class students and teacher. I didn't want them to know where I lived. What if they became frightened driving through the projects? Worse, what would they think of me? Would they talk about me when I left the car?

I didn't want to risk that they might judge me; I never even gave them a chance. Instead of giving my address, I cowardly gave directions to Michael's house, a friend of Eric. Eric had attended Bachelor Middle School and consequently had more white friends. He had a friend that lived in a neighborhood close to Charter Oak and that's where I instructed the teacher to drop me off, pretending it was my house.

Feigning tiredness, I felt myself withdrawing, building a solid shell like my turtle kindred spirit. I said my good-byes and slowly walked as if I was going to the house, praying desperately that the homeowners didn't see me. Mercifully, Ms. Levine pulled away before I had to drag the farce further.

Relief momentarily hit me, but then anguish and fear seeped in. It was night time and now I had to walk two miles to my house through an area that wasn't heavily populated. The residential area quickly ended on a bridge that crossed a canal leading to an area of small business warehouses that then led to the poorer side of town and the projects. Then I had to walk through the projects to get to my unit.

Elation ended in tears at my own stupidity and weakness. How could I be so vain? Would Mami find out and be furious at me? She was always very proud and worked extremely hard for all of us to be proud of ourselves and our heritage. I knew my history – I should have known better. I had let her down and put myself at risk. I felt like a *boba*. With tears of shame, compounded by the fear of walking alone at night, I walked the two miles to my house like a true *jibara*.

Welfare Queen

ONE OF THE greatest villains in the 1970s was the "welfare queen." Society had enough of supporting these women who were just having children to live extravagantly off the good, hard working tax payers. I'm not mocking these sentiments. The media does an excellent job of working people up and every generation needs their villain to blame for the economic injustices of the world. And yes, there are some who abuse the very systems that are there to help needy and worthy people. But I'm not here to go on a soap box but rather to introduce you to the worst welfare queen of Hartford, Connecticut – my mother.

The system had enough of these women, and my mother was the perfect example of the welfare queen who needed to be stopped. She became the poster child of a welfare queen in every news print, radio, and television news channel and the swift wheels of justice came down hard and publicly to end this abuse.

Let's pick up at the beginning. I've already shared how we ended up in Hartford with just the clothes on our back. However, officially Mami had a house in Bridgeport plus there was our trust fund from the Pedro Garcia Fund Drive. On paper it appeared as if we were rolling in money. The truth was that she horribly mismanaged her money. She gave away two houses as if she was giving away clothes that no longer fit her. When she came to Hartford, she was receiving social security benefits for the four children from my father, not including Rose. This income was not enough to support us.

She sought public assistance and explained her situation in full details. She was denied assistance because she was a property owner and had assets. A so-called friend then gave Mami the worst advice ever, advising her to lie and to not share the full story of her current financial struggle. Not making any excuses, she never should have lied; nevertheless, she did and she was granted food stamps and welfare. For two years, this is what paid the rent and fed us.

In a falling out with this friend, the friend decided to report Mami for welfare fraud and lo and behold Mami was arrested. I was ten years old. The newspaper and television crucified her saying how we were living in wealth. I don't know how you would define wealth but living in a rat-infested, cockroach infested ghetto certainly does not bring up that image to my mind.

We never had any excess. We lived for the 1st and for the 16th of the month when the food stamps would arrive, and we could go grocery shopping. In between, we stretched the food as best we could, bought food on credit, or turned to the church for their big government cheese and powder milk donations.

"Elizabeth, I need you to run to Shorty's." Aargh, those dreaded words from Mami! "Here's my list of what I need. Tell him to put it on credit."

"I went last time! It's Eric's turn," I whined.

I hated going to Shorty's to ask for credit. Shorty, a short African American man in his forties, kept a black composition book in a drawer near the cash register, where he tallied what we owed him. He was a sweet man, beloved by the community, but when he pulled-out "the notebook" in front of everyone, I just wanted to shrink away. Sometimes Mami would owe too much, leaving him little choice but to gently turn me away. It was always embarrassing.

We also shopped at the Goodwill Store before used clothes was considered vintage and trendy! Silvia and I would look all around before hopping out of the car and rushing into the store. The only new clothes we received were for the first day of school and Easter. I even had to drop-out of the Girl Scouts because I didn't have the money to purchase the required uniform. Furthermore, I never got to wear a beautiful white communion dress with a veil like Silvia did in Bridgeport. Now we were poor, so I had to do my communion with my school clothes!

We never went to the big American movie theaters, roller skating, bowling, zoo, a vacation, or simply dine out in a restaurant. At times we went to bed hungry. Snacks were a luxury. Food was just the basic staples, often just *arroz con leche*, a simple soup of rice with milk and salt.

Shopping with food stamps included putting up with the derision from the cashiers, who managed to roll their eyes and make snide comments. Christmas consisted of gifts from the Salvation Army, which of course were hand-made by the elves and thus they didn't come in the fancy packages. We were poor take my word for it.

It was a cold fall day - October 31, 1972. I had arrived from school and was looking forward to Halloween.

"*Nenas* (girls) come help me," Mami called. Rose, Silvia and I joined her in the kitchen where she sat with a big bag of candy corn and other hard candies. I reached for the individual pumpkin treat bags and began to stuff them with candies.

The excitement of preparing for Halloween was interrupted by a knock on the front door. It was too early for trick-or-treaters and few people ever used the front door. Silvia went and opened the door to two police officers. Startled, she rushed and got Mami.

Nervously and confused we stood back staring at the officers. I couldn't understand the conversation, but I did understand they were here to take Mami away. Silvia looked at me with huge frighten eyes. She ran to the kitchen and called my Titi Ana, who also lived in Charter Oak and quickly rushed over.

Mami was very quiet, but I could see the fear in her eyes. *"Nenas, esta bien,"* it's okay, she reassured us as she was led away.

We all surrounded Titi Ana and bombarded her with questions. Rose started to cry so I led her away to distract her. Titi Ana arranged to take us to *Abuela's* house in Bridgeport while she organized a collection for Mami's bail. Titi Ana, Luis (her boyfriend), and Silvia returned to Hartford to post bail and release Mami.

"She's out," *Abuela* shared. "They're heading back now."

"Yeah," I shouted as I translated for Rose, and we did a happy dance together.

It was a very cold day and patches of black ice covered the 95 South Expressway. As they neared a toll booth in New Haven, a city almost 30 minutes north of Bridgeport, Luis started to brake. The steering wheel pulled to the right and the car began to skid. Unable to control the car, it did a 360 degree turn and slammed right into the barrier of the toll booth.

Mami's whole body was thrown forward and her head smashed into the windshield. Shattered glass and blood splashed everywhere. Barely conscious, Mami groaned in the front seat. Stunned, everyone but Mami got out of the car. Mami lay her head back and that's when Titi Ana saw the cut in her eye. It was bleeding profusely down her face and body.

Abuela got the call that Mami was taken to the emergency room. It felt like an eternity as we waited to see what happened. We couldn't believe that another tragedy had struck.

"*Ven, vamos a rezar* (come, let's pray)." My *abuela* and *abuelo* gathered us together in her bedroom to pray while we waited for further news. Mercifully, she didn't lose her eye. When they finally walked through A*buela's* door, we all rushed over in relief. Silvia, uninjured, was terribly shaken and could barely speak. Luis brought in Mami's coat in a bag and took it to the tub, attempting to salvage it. It was so drenched in blood that you could barely recognize the original color of the coat. I stared as the tub water turned pink. No amount of rinsing was removing the blood; *Abuela* just threw it away.

Mami received the maximum sentence, six months in jail for fraudulently collecting $24,467. The State Welfare Commissioner lamented about the injustice of such a short sentence, "It's obvious the laws need to be changed and the penalty increased," he told the newspaper reporter. Mami was accused of having a savings account with $33,000 under the name of her children. Her husband, and previously described hero, was now "a man she lived with who died in an industrial accident." Lilly's medical needs were reduced to suffering from a hearing impairment. The house she negligently turned over to her mother and brother was subsequently sold but not by Mami, who never saw a cent of the reported $11,000 profit she made, plus the non-existent rent collection for two apartments that she never charged them for.

What they also failed to report was that this savings account was a Trust Fund that we could not use until we each turned 18 years old. Mami had fraudulently collected $13,032.09 in aid and $11,429.45 in health benefits. The state demanded that the money be recovered; thus, they took away Evi's, Eric's, most of Silvia's, and some of my trust fund to pay back the money she had fraudulently collected. This trust fund was supposed to be given to us when we turned 18 years old, the only remnant we had left of our father, and it was stripped away. I would have thought that it would have been protected. But it wasn't, and the innocent children were made to pay for her crime.

I don't know how or why, we were left alone in the projects. Eric was 13 years old and Rose was 5 years old. None of us knew how to cook, and we were afraid to let others know that we were alone. There was a live-in boyfriend at that time, but he was not our caretaker or responsible for us. We went to school every day hungry and scared to be discovered, like criminals.

I vividly remember one particular day. I was in fifth grade in Hooker Elementary School. It was lunch time and the loud bustle of the cafeteria surrounded me. The smell of the hot lunch filled the air. Children sat loudly on the tables releasing their pent up energy, talking and laughing. I was alone looking around. No longer being eligible for free lunch, I didn't have any lunch and didn't want to draw attention to myself. I picked an empty table and sat alone.

"Grrrr!" grumbled my stomach. Quickly I looked around hoping no one heard it.

"Grrrr!" persisted my stomach.

I was so hungry. I looked down avoiding any eye contact, but I could see everyone eating from the corner of my eyes. I felt alone and hungry, swallowing back the tears that were threatening to come. Mortified, I felt my tears inching out. As hard as I tried, I couldn't stop them. I was crying, trying desperately to bury my head as deeply as I could hoping not to be seen, wishing I could pull my head deep into my shell like a turtle.

"What's wrong?" asked a male teacher who noticed me.

"I'm hungry," I blurted out before I could even stop the words. Appalled, I broke down crying even more.

"Come," he said as he gently led me away to the teacher's lounge. He sat me down, pulled out his lunch, and gave me his sandwich. I barely looked at him but greedily grabbed the sandwich and wolfed it down. Though grateful, I was terribly embarrassed.

The pain of hunger left an emotional scar. Still today, I get an irrational, emotional response to hunger. Just ask my husband and children; they will eagerly share about my infamous break down at Burger King. After mass, my husband took us all to Burger King. However, I had skipped breakfast and a fast food burger is definitely not what I wanted. I burst out crying, and everyone had to march out of Burger King to get me properly fed with a hearty breakfast!

Besides hunger, I endured the humiliation of begging. Much to my chagrin, on some weekends my aunt stopped by and took us begging door to door or on street corners. One such time, it was my turn to go and knock on the door with my hand out asking for assistance. I knocked and nervously waited for the door to open. A woman opened the door, and I put out my hand asking for a hand-out. The woman quickly became very angry at my intrusion.

"You filthy spic (an ethnic slur)," she snarled at me, and proceeded to spit on me as if I was the biggest piece of trash she had ever seen. Trembling I wiped my face and walked away in utter disgrace.

My aunt would also take us to visit Mami in jail. We had to wait in a glass waiting room until the officer escorted Mami to the room. She wore prison clothes, her hair wasn't stylishly made up, and she wore no makeup. Despite this changed appearance, she always had a smile for us and provided a joyful visit for us. She'll tell us prison stories and proudly share her latest hobby, crocheting. I worried about her being bullied by other prisoners, but she would assure me that she was fine and had made lots of friends. I couldn't help but worry anyway.

At home, we all shared a great sense of responsibility for each other. One evening as we gathered around the kitchen table, someone knocked on our door. I went to take a peek and only saw a tall dark figure. I screamed hysterically, scaring the daylights out of Eric, and dove under the kitchen table. It turned out it was a priest, a friend of Mami, who came by to check on us. All I saw was the black garb against the dark evening. I never made it to his face. Well, we were caught now – I blew it.

The priest arranged for friends of Mami to take us in. Mind you, this family, the Martinez family, was just as poor as we were and there were nine of them. I have to say that such generosity was not uncommon, and this caring spirit is one that I always warmly remember and admire about our Puerto Rican community. The Martinez's were a good Catholic family for which I will forever be grateful for and pray that God will always bless them for their generosity. I know it wasn't easy for them to take us in. Eric, however, stayed behind. Lord only knows what this was like for him. At least Evi, who was not living with us at this time, would come and periodically stay with him.

We had to transfer to another school and adjust to this new living situation. The Martinez family had lots of children our age so there also were a lot of good times, especially for me, as I bonded with the oldest daughter. Her mad crush on Donny Osmond rivaled my own crush on Peter Brady, and it helped the time pass as we shared our daydreams.

Unfortunately, this was an especially hard time for Silvia. She was very proud and independent and at twelve years old she had the natural moodiness of adolescence. She ruled over me with an iron fist to make sure that I always was a good guest and not impose on their hospitality.

During our stay there, I lost a tooth. Excitedly, I placed it underneath the pillow.

"I hope I get fifty cents instead of a quarter. I'm going to buy a Chunky Bar," I thought, planning how I would use the money.

The morning sun sneaking through the curtain woke me up, and the first thing I did was lift my pillow looking to see what the tooth fairy, or *el ratoncito* as we called it in Spanish, left me. There was nothing there. I checked in between the pillow case and the pillow, but no it wasn't there either.

"Hmmm, could it had fallen?" I wondered as I jumped to the floor to look underneath the bed.

Exhausting my search efforts, I sat baffled on the bed.

"Oh my God, *el ratoncito* doesn't know where to find me."

Feeling completely disappointed, I cried, wishing I was back home with mami.

One morning on April Fool's Day, we were ready to go to school when Eric showed up. We were very excited to see him at the door, but he quickly blurted out that *Abuela* had died. Our initial reaction was, "ha, ha April Fool's – but that's not funny." So he again announced that *Abuela* died. We were hesitant to believe him, but his face told us it was real. Silvia started wailing, "no, no." I saw her run around crying in shock. In disbelief, I leaned back against the wall. My *abuela* was gone.

What could be more precious than a grandmother? *Abuela* always spoiled us. Every visit was filled with hugs, kisses, morsels of snacks snuck to me, a dollar tucked in my hand, and of course scrumptious dinners. Even when she was blind, she continued to try to cook. Sometimes the meals were inedible, but we would assure her that it was delicious like always. Reaching out to us, she would pat our heads and identify who we were. By the very end, she started to get dementia and struggled with remembering us. It was difficult to see the toll the prolonged battle with diabetes had on her. I couldn't believe that she had died and at that moment, I fervently wished that Mami was here.

They released Mami so that she could attend the funeral and then she had to report back. It was unbearably upsetting. Spending the extra days with her made the subsequent good-bye even harder. Fortunately, soon after the system decided to release her. The nightmare had come to an end.

Once home, the friend who turned her into the authorities, to my surprise, came asking for forgiveness. She never thought it would mean jail time. Mami immediately forgave her and continued the friendship as if nothing happened. She always believed in forgiveness, love, and charity, values that I cherish today.

Christmas that year was horrific. Not only did my *abuela's* death still linger over us, but when we went to put up our artificial tree, we found that all the ornaments were gone. Everything but the tree was stolen, including the gifts Mami had been slowly buying for us. We were robbed by our very own Grinch, my uncle!

Determined, we decided to decorate the tree by making paper snowflakes and popcorn streamers. Nothing was going to put a damper on our favorite holiday.

You must understand that Mami was the best Santa in the world. She loved every holiday and always made a big deal about them. Every Christmas she did something really creative to convince us that Santa was real. One year, Santa had to move the sofa to get in through the window, leaving huge, muddy boot prints all over the apartment. Another year, he accidently dropped a toy in our living room that belonged to another child.

Then there were the times that we would be out *de parrandas*. A *parranda* is when a group of friends and family gathers together to wake up and surprise another friend with music and singing. Then they would proceed to another house, and so on. It's the Puerto Rican version of Christmas caroling. After a long evening of *parrandas* or just after midnight mass, we would come home very late only to find to our utter amazement that Santa had already arrived. And, of course, Mami had never left our sight, thus we knew for sure that Santa existed.

Most of the times, we received a combination of new and used toys. Mami would regale us with tales of clumsy elves who made some of the toys (the used toys) and lazy elves who had to resort to buying new toys. Figuring out who got a bought toy versus a made toy was part of the joy as we squealed in happiness after each gift, which rarely included what we wrote on our Christmas list to Santa. Oh yes, she was tricky and the best Santa around.

But this year she did not have the means to provide toys for all of us. While, unbeknownst to me, she struggled with that reality, I still believed in Santa and eagerly awaited Christmas morning. In the morning, I made my usual sprint to the tree looking for my gifts, hoping to find a Baby Alive doll. Instead, I found a used green knit sweater and a letter from Santa:

> Dear Elizabeth,
>
> I am so sorry that I didn't get you your Baby Alive. I ran out of time and couldn't make all the gifts I needed. You are such a good girl, and I love you. I hope you understand. I promise to get you your favorite toy next year.
>
> Love Santa

Stunned, I sat staring at that letter. Santa would never write such a letter; he cannot be that rotten. Trembling, I fought back tears as comprehension hit me. I looked at Mami and forced a small smile on my face. I moved my attention to Rose, who luckily Santa was able to bring presents for, and continued our celebration.

Later, when we were alone, I hugged my mother, and we both cried profusely. She apologized for letting me down.

She loved filling all of our childhood fantasies, and this is not how she wanted Santa to end for me.

"It's okay Mami. I understand," I reassured her.

I felt horrible and selfish that she had gone through so much stress trying to get me a present. The welfare queen had been properly put in her place.

Lioness

I ALREADY SHARED how protective Mami was of us. Her protective nature was put to the test when she was fooling around with a married man named Pomale. One evening Mami ran to the local Kings Department store with my aunt. She was expecting Pomale and told us to have him wait for her. Pomale showed up and Silvia, who was 15 years old at the time, told him to come in and wait, that Mami would return shortly. Pomale asked Silvia if she could drive with him to Kings to find Mami because it was important that he speak to her. Silvia explained that Mami was going to be back any second, but he was persistent. She was a bit hesitant to be alone with him, but he kept insisting, reassuring Silvia that it would be a quick drive. Kings was only four to five miles away.

Finally, Silvia gave in to his pleas and hopped in the car with him. It was a hot summer day and the evening was still pretty warm. Silvia, who has always been very self-conscious and conservative, was wearing a spaghetti strap, black and white tube top with shorts. She rarely used tops that accentuated her small breasts but since she was in the house, she did.

"Take a right at the light," Silvia said as Pomale crossed the railroad tracks.

Ignoring her, he continued straight passed the lights towards a residential area. It was dusk and starting to get dark.

"I said take a right," Silvia quickly corrected him.

"I'm turning around," he said while still driving in the wrong direction.

What was he doing? Silvia looked around the quiet, deserted residential neighborhood where everyone was secured inside their homes. Her apprehension rapidly grew into fear when he turned into an empty driveway.

Reacting quickly she reached for the door handle, but he was faster in grabbing her hand and trapping her.

"What are you doing, take me home."

"Okay, but please don't scream. I just stopped because I want to tell you something. I want you to know that I'm only dating your mother because I just want to be near you. You are so beautiful."

Leaning in he kissed her. Silvia began to struggled, tears running down her face.

"Stop please, I want to go home. Stop!"

He was heavy against her, and she felt the door handle jamming into her back as she fruitlessly attempted to move further and further away from his vile kisses. His hand was brusquely roaming on her body, and he began to tug down her shirt.

With his hand exploring her young body, she was able to reach the door handle and opened the door.

"Help, help me!" she hollered as loud as she could.

Strong, sweaty hands pressed down on her mouth, smothering her cries and pulling her back in.

"Stop screaming or I'll kill you," he threatened. Silvia quieted down, stared at him in fear, and nodded her head.

"We're going to Kings so stop screaming," he hissed. He closed her door and began to drive away. But again, he intentionally took a wrong turn.

"I swear I'll jump out of the car if you don't take me home this minute," yelled Silvia.

She was still close enough to our apartment; she knew she could run back home as fast as she could. She just needed to get out of the car.

She opened the car, and he speeded up screaming, "Okay, okay. I'm taking you home, close the damn door NOW!"

He reversed direction and crossed the tracks towards our apartment. When he pulled in front of the apartment and Silvia moved to leave the car, he grabbed her again.

"Tell someone and I'll kill you, I swear. You remember that I'll be watching you. You better not tell your mother."

Silvia angrily jerked her arm free and rushed inside, with that threat echoing in her ears. She ran to the safety of her room.

The next day, Silvia walked downstairs and found that Pomale was there again. He was sitting with us looking at family pictures. Mami invited her to sit with us to look through the pictures. Self-consciously she perched herself on the couch, keeping a wary eye on him. She saw that Pomale picked up a wallet picture of her and pocketed the picture without anyone noticing it. She wanted to say something, but he stared at her, silencing her with his cold look.

All weekend Silvia struggled with what she should do. She kept the secret to herself, frightened by his threats. While she was waiting for the school bus, she saw him slowly drive by. He looked directly at her and pointed to his eyes, communicating that he was watching her. In a panic, Silvia rushed onto the bus, even more frightened than before.

That afternoon, when the bus dropped her off, he was waiting for her again threatening her with his mere presence. She saw him and ran all the way home. She spent the whole week in fear, but she still did not speak up. With the weekend here, she knew that he'll be back in the house.

"I have to tell someone, I MUST tell someone. He could kill me and no one will know he did it," she thought.

I was lying on the full-size bed that she and I shared doing my homework. Silvia sat quietly on the edge of the bed, but that was normal for her. I didn't pay her much mind.

"Elizabeth, I have to tell you something," she started. I listened in horror as she recounted what had happened.

"Oh my God, Silvia, you have to tell Mami," I quickly advised.

"No, I can't. What if she thinks I provoked him?" she asked, stubbornly shaking her head.

"She won't. Trust me. You have to tell her the truth," I urged.

"I can't. I'm scared."

"Let me do it. I'll tell her everything. You know he'll be here soon," I volunteered.

Relieved, she agreed. Closing the bedroom door behind me, I rushed downstairs to tell Mami. Eric was sitting in the living room watching television as I recounted what happened. Mami called Silvia down to confirm the story.

Mami unequivocally believed Silvia, no questions asked, which was such a relief to Silvia. Mami rarely got mad, but when she did, it was like a tempest. This short 4'11" woman became a force to be reckon with. At that moment, Pomale arrived before Mami had a chance to calm down. Immediately, all hell broke loose. She angrily confronted Pomale, who tried to deny the attack by shifting the blame to Silvia, claiming she had been flirting with him. What a mistake that was! Mami went berserk.

"How dare you accuse Silvia of anything! I know my daughter, and she's a decent girl. Don't you dare think that because she doesn't have a father she's fair game!"

She demanded that he return the stolen picture. When Pomale persisted in denying the attack, Mami jumped into action, and slapped him. Quickly, Eric joined in and they both attacked Pomale. Pomale managed to throw Silvia's picture to Mami and rushed out of the house.

Mami was livid to think that anyone had the nerve to *sobrepasarse* (cross a boundary) with her *nena* (little girl). He had crossed the line, touching that one sensitive button of Mami – the fact that we didn't have a father. God forbid that anyone thought she could not be both mother and father to us. She was a lioness protecting her cubs.

Once her anger subsided, she moved onto sorrow and remorse. Crying, she apologized to Silvia for ever dating such a man and exposing Silvia to such a frightful attack.

We never spoke about this again, until a year later when unsettling news reached us. After the softball season, Pomale left to Puerto Rico to follow his wife. Rumors spread throughout the league that Pomale was in prison for killing her. He thought she was having an affair so he not only killed her, but he also chopped her body up in pieces trying to hide the evidence.

We were all shocked and disturbed to think that Silvia was a target of his obsession and could easily have been his victim as well. It was unnerving, and we were grateful that he was out of our life for good.

Silvia

Reminiscing

SITTING AROUND THE kitchen table exchanging stories and memories in our family is quite different than in other families. Stories quickly involve moments of fright, hunger, death. We laugh like other families because that's all that you can do – laugh. Rarely outside of our family circle do we even engage in this type of reminiscing. After all, who would believe us?

<u>Burning Bed</u>

One favorite family story is about the day Evi and Silvia almost burned down our house in Bridgeport. One day Evi and Silvia, who were 12 and 9 years old respectively, decided to do some housecleaning. They decided to rearrange their bedroom furniture. As they moved their furniture, they unplugged the lamp. The bedroom became dark, and they needed to plug the lamp back in. With the bed in the way, they decided that Silvia could hold a candle underneath the bed, lighting the way for Evi to find the socket. Silvia crawled under the bed with the lighted candle, while Evi fumbled around in search of the socket.

Silvia saw that the candle flames caught on the mattress. Initially, instead of fear, she was mesmerized by the red and yellow sparks. However, the flames seem to become alive and started spreading on the box spring. Realizing what was happening, Evi and Silvia did a mad dash out from under the bed. They ran to the kitchen to get pots of water to throw on the flames. Instead of extinguishing the flames, it started to spread. Not knowing what else to do, Silvia ran to the neighbors for help. They hurried back but it was too late; the mattress was engulfed in flames. The neighbors had no choice but to hoist the mattress over the window.

Mami got the call from the neighbors and terrified she rushed home. Poor Evi and Silvia received a spanking right in front of everyone.

Holidays

Mami loved the holidays and filled them with great memories for us. Besides Christmas, Mami loved Halloween. She loved seeing the little children dressed up in their costumes. Mami thought it was hilarious to have children do tricks for their treats. Therefore, she sometimes would have children bob for apples for extra treats. It was amazing how many kids volunteered and loved it. As for us, we rarely bought costumes. Rather, we made ourselves up, using her make-up, clothes, and creativity.

We also wouldn't go trick or treating in our own neighborhood. Mami would load us up in the car and drive us to middle class neighborhoods. When we finished there, she would then drive us to her favorite bar, *La Taverna de La Esquina* (The Corner Bar), where we collected change from the bar patrons. We thought this was super cool on top of our candy collection.

One Fourth of July was especially memorable. Mami had planned for us to go to Barkhamsted Lake. Going to the beach or the lake was always a big deal. In order to beat the crowds, we had to wake up around 5:00 a.m. I couldn't wait and didn't mind getting up so early. But I awoke to torrential rains.

"Let's go anyway. It'll stop," I tried to persuade Mami with my youthful optimism.

Mami was disappointed as well since she had looked forward to this outing just as much as we did. Determined not to let a little rain spoil our fun, she got the most ingenious idea.

Our living room was empty because Mami had discarded her old furniture. After being released from prison, she didn't want any reminder of the past. Since the living room was empty, Mami decided to convert our living room into our own beach.

She bought a plastic children's pool and put it right in the center of our living room and filled it up. We had our towels, beach toys, and cooler with food all set up. She then invited other neighborhood kids, and we had the best fun-filled day at "the lake" after all.

Adventure

We were not strangers to hitchhiking. Typically, we would hitchhike to the park to get to the softball games. However, there was one time when we went to Mountain Park, an amusement park, in Holyoke, Massachusetts. We went with a boyfriend of Mami's. Once there, they got into a fight over something and started arguing. Angry, he decided to take off and left us stranded.

Mami did not panic. With bravado, she assured us we will get home fine. In fact, we were going to have an adventure and hitchhike back. Excitedly, we would stick out our thumbs waiting for someone to stop. It was quickly apparent that no one was going to pick up a woman with four children.

"Hide behind the trees and don't come out until I say so," she instructed.

Soon a man stopped, an off duty police officer. Mami approached him, and he agreed to bring her back to Hartford. She then gave us the signal and out popped four scrambling children. He was taken aback and was not too happy. But he felt committed, and we all piled into the back seat. However, he decided that our presence wasn't going to stop him from trying to seduce Mami. During the whole ride, he flirted and caressed her neck and legs. It was so uncomfortable, and I was so disappointed to see a police officer behaving just like all the other men who constantly lusted after my mother.

Working Days

Mami had severe asthma. She was allergic to dust and pets. A change in weather and, of course, stress would trigger a bad asthma attack. When she got an attack, her eyes bulged and she'd gasp for air. One of us would run and get anything to fan her with, an album cover or a notebook. As one of us fanned her, the other would run for her asthma spray. She would sit in the chair, panting and wheezing, unable to speak, taking two pumps from her spray and inhaling the medicine deeply until the attack subsided. It was frightening to see her so weak and helpless, dependent on us for a simple breath. What would happen to her if any of us weren't there to get her inhaler? It was a frightening thought.

Because of her asthma, she never worked. However, once she took a job as a housekeeper for the Hartford Hotel. The Hartford Hotel was a hotel in the outskirts of downtown that catered to what constituted our homeless community. The hotel included one night renters and monthly renters. Many were alcoholic, schizophrenic, lonely, abandoned people. To others, the residents were scary, but to Mami they represented individual stories of interesting people. She loved meeting them, talking to them, learning about their history, and just enjoying their idiosyncrasies, especially the hoarders that accumulated a pile of bizarre and unexpected "treasures."

Sometimes she would take me with her. The first thing she did was get her list of rooms for the day. She had a master key, which I was allowed to carry. I could also help her to replenish the cleaning cart with linens and cleaning products. Then I got to push the cart down the corridors. Topping the day's excitement was when she was left a stack of coins as a tip. The job didn't last long because the hotel was closed and torn down. After this, she took a job at a department store. That job lasted one day, and she never took another job in her life.

La Baby

Rose was the baby of the house. She had beautiful curly black hair, with dark big eyes and a dimple on her chin. She had a lot of energy, and clumsily, would prance around shaking the house with her pounding footsteps.

"Elizabet, Elizabet," she hollered, mispronouncing my name, and diving into my arms, knocking my breath away, excitedly telling me about her day.

Due to her hearing impairment, she spoke very loudly and was a little clueless to everything around her, interrupting as needed, demanding my attention. Like Lilly before her, Mami imposed little discipline on her. Rose had no chores and could come and go as she pleased from our neighbor's apartment.

At five years old, Mami still gave her chocolate milk in a bottle, cherishing her baby girl, while we rolled our eyes in disgust.

Like us, she loved music. Feeling the vibrations from the floor, she danced away in the living room to her own rhythms, bringing us great laughter and joy.

One summer day, I was sitting in the stoop watching her run around in our yard with our cousin, Anthony. Suddenly her ankle twisted and she fell. I ran over to check on her and saw her elbow grotesquely protruding out, in a bizarre position. She had broken her arm.

Our baby girl spent a week in the hospital in an arm sling.

Surrogate Brother

Eric, being surrounded by so many sisters, was stuck with puny me as his wrestling partner. Eric loved martial arts and would use me as a sparring partner, which of course quickly disintegrated into an all out wrestling match. We would clear a space from the living room. Pushing furniture to the side, we created a wrestling ring.

"Try to hit me," he'll taunt, blocking my punches and sneaking a slap to my head. We circled each other vying for position and for an opportunity to land a blow. He'll stand in his karate stance while I rushed in to tackle him. He liked to flip me, which worked just fine with me as sparring standing was a losing position for me anyway. If he didn't flip me, I would head butt him straight in his gut trying to knock him down as fast as I could. When he reached around my waist to stop me, I'll buckle my knees letting my dead weight bring us both down. Squirming, I could then resort to dirty fighting, scratching, biting, pulling hair, squeezing my skinny legs on his waist trying to create a vise grip. No fancy moves for me! Exhausted or until someone screamed uncle, we would leave a trail of bruises and scratches on each other.

We loved Bruce Lee and Sonny Chiba. Eric would take me to the Colonial, a small movie theater that featured karate flicks. No sooner than we arrived back home, the jostling and fighting would resume.

Besides wrestling, I was also the one he would persuade to stay up all night to see the sunrise or walk the railroad tracks in search of animal bones. Whenever I woke up from a nightmare, it was into his bed that I crawled into. I loved being his surrogate little brother.

As a boy, and the only boy at that, he had free rein. He could come and go as he pleased as long as he was honest to Mami. That was her only rule for him – nothing behind her back. He survived by spending as much time away from the projects as possible, and he was the only one that lived amongst the mainstream world, beyond our front stoop. But at 18-years old that world turned against him.

His 16 year-old white girlfriend became pregnant. I was ecstatic and thrilled as the delivery day neared. Two days before, I welcomed my first nephew from Evi. I was on a high to be an aunt and eager to welcome my next niece or nephew. The news that Eric's girlfriend was giving birth came, and we hurried to the hospital, excited to see the new baby. He was a beautiful, big baby boy that looked just like Eric.

We crowded the room eager to hold him only to find a room filled with tears; the baby was to be given up for adoption. Eric's hand was forced; forfeit his rights or face statutory rape charges.

No one prepared me for this news. I felt like I was on an amusement ride, which unexpectedly plummeted me down a terrifying high drop. One moment I was filled with excitement and anticipation then the next I was left speechless as I was unexpectedly plunged down. Unfortunately, there were no squeals of delight at the end of the "ride"; I was just left stunned.

Thereafter, I always thought of him, searching every stranger's face for a glimpse of recognition. For 20 years I dreamed of reuniting with him, picturing his face, and mostly praying for him. I had to believe that it was the best thing for him, even though it was a great loss for me.

Finally, I was blessed with the opportunity to meet him. I already had moved to Miami and was visiting Connecticut for Christmas. Eric called us from Oklahoma to share the news. His firstborn son had tracked down his birth mother and wanted to meet us. Ecstatically, we all gathered at Silvia's house, eagerly waiting for his arrival. I couldn't believe that he actually found us. At last this handsome brave man was standing before my eyes. He had our dark blond/light brown curly hair. Immediately I could see the strong resemblance to Eric. He had his nose and most notably his lips, which tends to smirks in a funny smile. My heart lurched at the uncanny similarity. Then as we started getting acquainted, the similarities grew and grew. I could see my precious brother in him.

Without scaring the poor man, I just wanted to hug him and never let him go. I'm forever grateful to his adoptive family for bringing up a wonderful young man, and I thank God that we were reunited. He's since married and has two lovely girls, and we continue to stay in touch. God works such great miracles.

Eric and me at Mansfield Training School

Turn To the Grim

AS YOU CAN see, memories start taking a turn to the grim. The most popular family theme in our family is death. Death was a family friend, well known and expected. There was very little illusion that death is something that happen to others or that I have a lifetime before me. I clearly learned that life is precious and not to be wasted. This lesson was drilled into me with each agonizing death. It was not uncommon for us to sit around predicting and betting on who was the next to go. For a long time, the oldest person in our family lived to be only 53 years old.

My father's death started the parade of deaths. His sister committed suicide. I never knew this aunt, but I just heard the story of the tragedies surrounding the Garcia family, and I'm not sure if she died before or after my father.

I do, however, remember the death of his brother, Fay. I remember attending the wake and seeing his wife and children crying. They were my age, around six and seven years old. Fay also died a hero's death. In his case, he was out boating with his family when the boat overturned. He rescued his wife and two children from drowning but had nothing left to rescue himself. He drowned, too exhausted to make it to safety.

Then there was the death of my aunt Nubia. Nubia was the coolest aunt. She had long brown hair that hung all the way down to her butt. She wore flower skirts – a real flower child. She was born with a congenital heart problem and was not expected to live very long. She actually made it to 24 years old, defying the doctor's expectations. No wonder I thought she was so cool; she was young and full of energy.

Whenever I slept over her house, all I could hear was her pacemaker. She was very open about her condition, and didn't mind my youthful curiosity as I stared at the red, thick scar that cut across her chest. She even encouraged me to touch it and answered all my questions.

Her apartment was always filled with music, psychedelic lights, beaded curtains, and, of course, drugs. I would sit in her kitchen in a thick fog of marijuana smoke, enjoying her silliness and giggles. She was very sweet and full of life, living recklessly trying to defy death. When she died, she left three young children.

After Nubia, Pizza, a step-uncle, died. Pizza was a transvestite whom I only knew as a woman. She had a long-time partner who apparently fell in love before realizing she was a he. After giving him a beating, he decided to stay with her just the same, and they lived together for many years. The funeral home would not honor the family wishes to bury her as a woman. No one knew her as a man, thus it was a shocker to attend a wake for Pedro instead.

My grandmother died while Mami was in prison. *Abuela* was only 53 years old, but she appeared to be 70 years old. She had uncontrolled diabetes, which in the end left her blind and with dementia.

Abuela had a tough life. At 14 years old she was married off to the town's rich man, a 62 year old widower who happened to be her brother-in-law. She had two children with him (Josephina and Elizabeth, my mother). She was miserable and eager to leave him. Taking the first opportunity to leave her town of Camuy, she ran away with Musa, the father of the rest of her six children. Little did she know that she jumped from the frying pan into the fire. This turned out to be a violent and unhappy relationship.

Courageously, she left Puerto Rico on her own when Mami was around eleven years old. Mami was suffering from severe asthma and was very sickly in Puerto Rico; therefore, moving was an added incentive. She moved alone to New York and eventually moved to Bridgeport where she had some cousins.

My *abuela* finally left her second husband and married the man I considered to be my *abuelo*, Rogelio. He was a younger man and was very good to her. He shared her faith, took care of her when she was sick, and stood by her side when her children challenged her. He played the guitar and loved to make movies. In my eyes, he looked like a movie star, very handsome and distinguished with his straight black hair and dark eyes.

My greatest sadness is that when A*buela* died, it was as if he died as well. I never saw or heard from him again, nor did I ever have the chance to say good-bye. He just disappeared out of my life, like a puff of air in a magic show. Poof - here today gone tomorrow, leaving another hole in my heart.

Abuela's death was followed by the murder of my cousin, Cha-Cha. Cha-Cha was only 13 years old. There were three cousins of the same age: Terri, Cha-Cha, and me. We were quite a trio whenever we got together. Cha-Cha was the youngest of the trio, a skinny brunette full of smiles – her favorite way of greeting you was sticking out her tongue and making her funny faces. She was giggly and mischievous, always a lot of fun to be with, and most importantly she brought out my youthful side.

It's strange to say that, because I was young. Yet I wasn't. Too many deaths, chaos, and changes had chipped away at any childhood illusions; there never were any rose colored glasses for me. I was too mature for my age, too cautious, too serious, too responsible. In fact, I clearly remember one morning, waking up terribly perturbed by my dream. I dreamt I went to bed as a ten year old and woke up a woman. Cha-Cha knew how to make me laugh and be a child again.

One Christmas morning we were visiting Dolly, Cha-Cha's older sister who had moved to Hartford. Dolly had been battling drug addiction since I'd known her. We were proud of her for moving away from Bridgeport, being clean from drugs, and maintaining her own apartment. This was a very rare visit celebrating her recovery. She looked beautiful, healthy, and proud. (It turned out not to be permanent.

Eventually she returned to drugs and became a notorious gang leader).

This day, however, was a day of celebrating the positive. She was finally clean and doing really well. The television was on in the background when the news of a murdered teenager in Bridgeport caught our attention. It was Cha-Cha. We could see her body being carried away on a stretcher.

On Christmas Eve, Cha-Cha went out dancing with her sister, Lizzie, and our cousin, Terri. It was already after midnight, and she was ready to go home. Because Lizzie and Terri were not ready to leave, they arranged for an acquaintance to take Cha-Cha home. Instead of Cha-Cha being safely driven home, she was raped, strangled, and left naked in the snow. The murderer was never caught and a mystery remains as to who ended up taking her home. They arrested the original person who was asked to take her home, but he was cleared of all charges.

How do you even digest such brutality? She was such a vibrant young girl, a bright light snuffed off way too soon. I couldn't help but feel vulnerable. I'd already known about rape, but it hitting so close to home made it even more real. There was an instant protective reaction across the family. The lectures about the dangers of men were all revisited. My cousin, Terri, whom I also was very closed to, in fact, she was the closest thing to a confidante that I ever had, was shipped off to some type of reform school and that was the end of the trio.

Cha-Cha and Me

Cha-Cha's death devastated her mother who never fully recovered. At times she lived in her own world where she talked to Cha-Cha as if she was still alive. It was eerie and sad to visit with her and see her cooking over her stove having a full conversation with Cha-Cha, laughing as if Cha-Cha was right there performing her silly antics. It's true what they say: a parent should never have to bury his or her own children.

Tragedy struck yet again, and she had to live through burying two more of her children. Lizzie and Cano, both young in their twenties, were drug addicts and using prostitution to feed their habit. Cano, a handsome teenager with blond hair and green eyes, who spent hours playing with me, contracted AIDS. I was sorry to hear that he fell into the trap of drug addiction.

Lizzie also passed away from AIDS. I was never close to her. I found her a little intimidating. Her brother Juni speaks lovingly of her as he shared his memories of Lizzie.

"Lizzie always felt rejected and never recovered from the separation of our parents" he explained.

Once she got into drugs, she was completely entrapped in a negative life style to support her habit. She ended up having six children from different men. Her mother and sister had to assume responsibility for these children. She finally also contracted AIDS and died one year after Cano.

Juni was very fortunate because although he too began to dabble with cocaine, he said he once got a vision of Cano telling him, "Just leave it alone." Juni got so freaked out that he ran and flushed the drugs and never went back to them.

He was the one brother that managed to stay away from drugs and crimes. Today, he is proud that he has finally learned to read and is giving his children and grandchildren the stability that he lacked. It was difficult for him to be illiterate and not to be able to read to his children. He now has the pleasure of cuddling with his grandchildren and reading them a story. Plus, he is so happy that he is able to read his Bible. I thank God that he survived.

His mother had to live through these tragedies as best she could. She was always the sickly aunt - the one that I always bet on to be the next to go. Yet she outlived many others, finally passing away from her diabetes at 52 years old.

Between these family deaths, which literally were occurring once a year, friends were also dying. Mami was friends with our neighbor who happened to be mute. Sadly, I don't even know his name as he was simply called *El Mudo* – the mute. He strived to fit in by being the light of a party, a little like the class clown, and would drink heavily. Behind the happy face, however, dwelled a depressed young man who committed suicide by hanging himself in his living room. I remember Mami hurrying across the street to join several people who tried to hold him up, but it was too late.

At that time, I had just started a friendship with a girl at school, a rare occurrence for me. Like me, she had a sibling, a brother, with special needs. That commonality created a bond between us. She and I did not like gym classes, where we were relegated to play alone off to one side. So instead, we would periodically sneak off to play in the swings in the adjacent park. One day I was waiting for her to sneak off, but she never showed up to gym class. Bummed that I had to stay in gym class, I wondered what happened. Soon I heard that the day before, her brother was playing with a gun and shot her in the head. That was the last time that I tried to befriend anyone in school – I stuck to mere acquaintances after that.

Yes, stories take a turn to the grim in my family. Besides death, criminality is the next pervasive theme. I've already alluded to drugs, prostitution, and gangs – all present and accounted for in my extended family. I was quite experienced in rolling joints even though I have never taken a whiff of marijuana my entire life.

Stealing was the next notorious presence in my family. Even my *abuela*, blinded by her diabetes, would walk in a grocery store and steal as if no one could see her. It was actually funny.

"*Me vieron* (did they see me)?" she'd ask as she shoved an item into her clothing. Of course, she was usually seen; after all how effective of a thief can she be being blind! I would pay for the items at the cashier and let her think she got away with it.

I have an uncle and cousin that I barely knew since they spent most of their life in prison for one robbery after another. Whenever a family member came to visit us, we were placed on top alert to make sure we were not robbed by them.

Gifts to me were more than likely stolen. My last stolen gifts were when I went off to college. *Negro*, my uncle, was excited that I was going away to college. He presented me with a lovely white soft robe with Clinique make-up, all stolen from someone's house. I was truly touched that he thought of me, but like always, I was appalled the items were stolen. My only consolation was that all this was coming to an end, and I was moving away from the craziness.

This particular uncle eventually was repeatedly arrested for child molestation. He was always a kind uncle, but as soon as Mami died the tenuous boundary was broken, and he attempted to kiss me on the lips. It's so sad because each family member, despite their particular issues, also had goodness in them. There were a lot of moments of laughter, kindness, and love. This uncle, for instance, instilled a love of cooking in me. We rarely celebrated holidays with the family but on those occasions that we did, he was the one that cooked all the traditional Puerto Rican dishes such as the *pasteles* (similar to a meat tamale but made from root vegetables instead of corn meal) and *pudin de pan* (bread pudding).

With my aunt, I developed the love of roller coasters. She was a daredevil who always made me feel secure. She was strong and would hold me in her arms as we ran from one thrilling ride to another. She encouraged me to take risks and not to be afraid. Most importantly, I love her dearly because I know Mami loved her and they were very close and much alike. Like Mami, she struggled with drinking. Mami's death hit her hard. She always gave us lots of love, showering us with hugs and kisses.

My dysfunctional family was great for teaching the complexity of life. Life certainly would be easier if we could simply vilify someone and make them all bad, but there's no such thing. The goodness will always shine through as well. Unfortunately, I was better at avoidance and running away. I severed relationships with many family members out of fear of not knowing how to balance my old life with the new one I desired. I feared chaos and bringing unwanted drama to my life. Without Mami to serve as a protective barrier, I could only run away. I pray for forgiveness. Despite my distance, I do treasure the good times that they gave me. Those times are not forgotten.

Lest you're left with an impression that my entire family was dysfunctional, let me introduce you to my mother's two younger brothers who began breaking the mold. One brother was always the religious one. He did this dance routine with a handkerchief that would have everyone laughing in stitches. You could not help but laugh when you were around Felo. He frequently took us to his church services. Unlike us, he wasn't Catholic. He went to a Pentecostal church, which was always filled with great music and a celebration of the Holy Spirit. This God-loving uncle had one initial bad first marriage but then divorced and led a new life with a wonderful Christian family.

Then the baby of the family, Uncle Hector, was the hard working, goal oriented brother. He assumed guardianship of Nubia's three children, went on to marry and have three girls of his own, and was the first middle class member of our family. He was the only adult I knew that kept a steady job and bought his own house. He even took vacations! He epitomized the hard-working father who did everything to steer his family in the right direction, and he raised six wonderful children. I've maintained relationships with both of them. My *abuela* would be very proud of them.

Contradictions

MY CHILDHOOD WAS far from normal. It certainly was nothing like "Leave It To Beaver" or "The Brady Bunch." My life was full of contradictions. I quickly learned that life is not black and white, but rather that there are a lot of gray areas.

I was raised a good Catholic. Mami loved Jesus and did all she could to pass down Catholic values to us. I went to church, did all of my sacraments, and was active in the youth group. Our house was a typical Catholic home with a special corner set up as an altar, ready for lit candles and prayer petitions. There we had a statue of the Virgin Mary, *La Milagrosa* (my confirmation saint), wearing a light blue gown and standing on a serpent. We also had a bust of Jesus with the crown of thorns. A two-dimensional wood carving of the image of the sacred heart of Jesus adorned our living room wall. Jesus' eyes in this carving gave you the impression of being constantly looked at no matter where you sat in the room, making us constantly play musical chair to see if His eyes were still following us. Lastly, my favorite image was in her bedroom. It was of the Guardian Angel watching over a boy and girl crossing a bridge.

We observed religious traditions, with my favorite being Good Friday, a day that we spent in solemn observance of our Lord's sacrifice. It is a day of contemplation of the incredible love of Jesus Christ, who willingly gave his life for me. On this day there was no working, dancing, cleaning, watching television, or listening to music. We would see a movie about Jesus and then participate in the yearly Good Friday procession. The procession consisted of praying the 14 Stations of the Cross around the neighborhood and singing hymns and saying prayers. At times, Silvia and I had the privilege of reading one of the prayers or reflections for a station.

My *abuela* was also very religious. She'd coax me over to pull her gray hairs while she read me the Bible. Although we were Catholic, Mami exposed us to other denominations. She wanted us to know that God is everywhere, so we sporadically went to Pentecostal, Lutheran, and Black Baptist services. Her philosophy was simply to walk into any church and pray. For me it was great to see the various styles of worship, from the Catholic services filled with comforting, familiar rituals, to the music-filled black gospel services, to the revival-style filled with the Holy Spirit services of the Pentecostal. Being a Catholic where services were more solemn, I would get startled and frightened when all of a sudden someone would leap up in the air filled with the Holy Spirit. Not only would they leap in joy, but some would start talking in tongues, while others fell to the floor crying in surrender. It was a different experience, and I'm glad I was exposed to the various forms of worship.

At one point, Mami got the notion to pray to Buddha. She bought a little black Buddha and placed it in a place of honor. Very soon, however, she took a hammer to the Buddha and smashed it to smithereens when she found herself in the midst of a personal crisis. Thus, she reverted back to her Catholicism.

She taught us and encouraged Christian values. Mami stressed the importance of forgiveness, charity, and being loving. She loved how Jesus befriended women, children, and tax collectors. His acceptance of everyone is something she sought to teach us. I always say that her greatest gift to me was passing her Catholic faith. Little did she know how her faith made me strong and prepared me to survive the storms in my life.

From this faith came her desire to see her daughters marry as virgins, in white dresses, in the Catholic Church. That was the pinnacle of success for a woman. Our virginity was our prized possession.

One day, when I was around 12 or 13 years old, I was riding my bicycle. It was a boy's bike so it had a bar down the middle. Suddenly swerving on a patch of pebbles, I lost my balance and landed between the bar. Sore I rode back home, expecting Mami's comfort.

"What, I can't believe it!" she raged at me when she saw I had a spot of blood. "You lost your virginity. I could kill you; I'm so mad at you!"

She ranted and ranted and finally punished me to my room. Completely bewildered, I couldn't understand how I lost my virginity and was now reduced to "spoiled goods." According to Mami, you were "unmarriageable" if you were not a virgin.

"What does she mean? I just fell." I asked Silvia really worried at what I had done that was so horrible.

With no clear answers, I took small comfort that at least I wasn't taken to the doctor to ensure that I was still a virgin as she threatened to do.

Despite her strong religious values, here's the contradiction – as much as she loved Jesus, she failed to truly trust Him and turn to Him for fulfillment. I always say that she reminded me of the Samaritan woman in the Bible. The Samaritan woman was thirsty and sought to quench her thirst through multiple marriages, not realizing that true fulfillment only comes through a relationship with God.

In Mami's case, fulfillment came by turning to men and alcohol. She was a very lonely woman on a quest to find us a father. How I hated when she would say that. I don't quite know how to explain this part of her life. I can only just say it. Mami had an unhealthy relationship with men and sex, her Achilles Heel.

She explained it best, "At 24, young and pretty, I was widowed. Men never loved me. Only Pellin loved me. The rest only loved me for my youth and my looks. Now they love me to live off of me or for sex...they only seek pleasure – and I suffer; nobody truly loved me...I suffer quietly and drinking…I'm practically an old bum." After her death, we found these heart-wrenching sentiments expressed in a letter she had written to us.

She suffered and drowned her sorrows in drink and behind a happy face. The more she was with men, the more unworthy she felt, the more she drank, and the more she pulled away from the church. She went from maintaining a friendship with our local priest to eventually not going to church altogether, only sending us on our own. Not only was she hard on herself, but parts of the church community was also hard on her and us.

If we stayed behind in the hospitality room or participated in a church social event, we would occasionally get an evil eye from those who judged Mami. As we walked by, I would hear the whispering and snickering. When we sat at a table, with a cold politeness, someone would move somewhere else.

"*Ignoralo* (ignore them)," Mami would tell us, but it still hurt.

The polite façade, however, came crumbling down when I was around 14 years old and had my first experience with puppy love. I had participated in a youth group retreat where I spent time with Jose, one of the youth group members. He was tall, good-looking, and easy to talk to, the kind of guy who easily befriended girls with their more sensitive side.

Every moment I could, I managed to be near him. He, too, sought my company. We sat together at each gathering, sharing our inner-most thoughts. Maybe because we were on a retreat, we engaged in deep philosophical conversations that transcended your typical adolescent talks. A bond was blossoming between us.

Talking progressed to holding hands as we walked together between visits to the various shrines and cathedrals. Finishing our walk through before everyone else, we went outside and sat together waiting for the group to catch up with us. He pulled me close to his chest, and I leaned my head on his shoulder, enjoying my first experience with a boy.

He's so perfect, I thought: funny, respectful, and we shared the same perspectives and values. On the bus drive back, we sat together, and he put his arm over me and held my hand the entire drive back. It felt wonderful.

"I've had a great weekend with you," he whispered to me.

"Me too."

"I don't want it to end."

"I know."

"Maybe you could be my girlfriend?"

Those tentative words brought a great smile to my face. I couldn't believe it, and of course, I did want to be his girlfriend. I thought he was fantastic.

"Yes, I'll love that but I have to ask Mami first."

"I understand. I have to ask my mom as well."

When Mami came to pick me up at the church, I was giddy with excitement, eager to share the news with her.

"Mami, you won't believe what happened. Jose asked me to be his girlfriend."

Mami knew Jose from church, and she was tickled to see me infatuated with my first puppy love. After teasing me and pumping me for all the details, she gave me a big hug and her blessings. My first boyfriend; wow, I was so happy.

I had to wait a couple of days to see Jose again at the youth group meeting. Wednesday evening came, and I couldn't wait to see him. Dressing that evening, I took extra steps with my hair and picking my clothes. When I arrived, I looked for him but he wasn't there yet. I turned my head looking at each new arrival, eager to see him.

Finally, he walked in. Straining to make eye contact, I sent a bright smile across the room. I got a barely perceptible nod, and he turned and approached a group of his friends. He didn't rush up to me; in fact, he avoided me and sat away from me when the meeting started. I immediately felt awkward and unsure of myself. The easy camaraderie we shared had dissipated.

I had to wait for the meeting to finish, anxiously fidgeting, before he finally approached me. I tried to resurrect the connection we shared by smiling and joking.

"Hey, Mami said yes. We could go out," I shyly shared.

He shuffled awkwardly, and fumbled his words. He hastily told me that his mother was furious with him. She vehemently prohibited him to go out with me.

"I'm sorry but Mami says your mother is a whore, and she doesn't want me associating with you," he explained.

"She says you're all whores. She's really mad at me; I just can't go out with you."

I blinked in surprise, standing there like a fool, totally dumbfounded not knowing how to reply. Taking advantage of my total immobilization of brain and mouth, he made a quick apology and rushed off, leaving me there profoundly wounded. I didn't cry because I was too proud, but the wound cut deep into my young innocent heart.

But, back to Mami. Mami was a very beautiful, sexy woman. She was petite at 4 feet 11 inches. She had brown hair that she would dye red. She was very busty and flirtatious. Her greatest feature was her large brown eyes that spoke volumes. Whenever she walked in a room, she was the center of attention. She loved dancing, laughing, drinking, and soaking in the attention. She was most comfortable with men, and they radiated towards her like moths to light. Mami put all her identity in her sexuality – she let it define her and define her self-worth. Unfortunately, each failed encountered just ate away at her self esteem and led her to more drinking. It was a vicious cycle.

There would be days that I could wake up to breakfast across a total stranger that she picked up or a stranger in the living room that she felt sorry for and brought home to offer shelter and a meal. That captures the dichotomy of her nature.

Much of our life was one great big party. Every Saturday and Sunday during the summer we went to the local softball games. There were two local leagues, one that played on Saturday at Colts Park and one that played on Sundays in *el parque de las piedras* (the stone-wall park). I loved the game, cheering enthusiastically and discussing strategy with the team manager, who indulged my youthful exuberance.

The games were a big community event. Local vendors would sell their *piraguas* (shaved ice), *frituras* (Puerto Rican fritters), sodas, and ice cream. After the games, the team would go to a local club for drinks and music.

During the winter, we went to the Dominoes Club, where teams competed against each other. Again, I loved the game, rooting for my favorite contender, discussing strategy, and learning the game. When we were not playing Dominoes, we would go to El Lyric, the local Spanish-speaking theater. I loved to see the Mexican folk hero, *Santo, El Mascarado de Plata*, who was a silver-masked wrestler who fought for justice.

Whether it was the park, the dominoes games, or the movies, we ended the evening by rushing home to bathe, change, and start part two of the day. With one bathroom, we had the process down to a science. We all could bathe and dress and be ready in 30 minutes flat if need be. We would rush and be out the door again, sometimes leaving Rose with the neighbors.

There were numerous Latin clubs that featured local salsa bands. We were always among the first to arrive that way Mami could talk her way in, and we could grab the best seat in the house, upfront closest to the dance floor. We danced the night away. Men would come ask us to dance and, if they didn't, Silvia, Mami and I would dance together, which often led to a group of men coming up to dance with us.

Mami drank heavily and flirted outrageously.   Men, however, knew Silvia and I were off-limits.   She always managed to make that point clear.   Sometimes the clubs would become a hotbed for fights, and we'd have to rush out a side door to avoid the fights and eventually find another club with a different crowd.

At other times, professional performers would come to town, and we would rush to see every one of them: Celia Cruz, El Gran Combo, Johnny Ventura, Willie Colon, Fania All Stars and many more.   With Mami's charm, connections, and flirtations, we also got to personally meet some of them.

After dancing the night away, we were up bright and early the next day to start all over again.   In addition to the clubs, Mami would never hesitate to crash weddings or house parties.   At times we got away with it, but at other times we were caught and kicked out.

"Who let that whore in here?   Get her out."

It was humiliating, especially as I could see the commotion starting, the looks directed our way, the rush to the kitchen to confront the homeowner, the steady walk towards."

"Self-righteous hypocrite," Mami would say, pretending that it didn't faze her as she reached for another beer, numbing herself to the insults.

Being with Mami was like being with a wild, out-of-control friend. We danced, joked, and enjoyed each other's company, while at the same time a touch of fear of things catching up with you settled in your stomach.

In the meantime, I would stay up with her sharing stories, laughing, and talking about guys who caught our eyes. I could tell her anything, and she was fairly candid with me as well.

If men radiated to Mami like moths to a light, many women abhorred her and by extension, us. We were called, "*Elisa y sus putas*" – Elisa and her whores. People assumed that my sister and I were also drinking and having sex, which could not be further from the truth.

Mami lived by a strict motto, "Do as I say, not as I do." She never pretended that what she did was right; she was her own harshest critic, especially when she was tipsy or drunk. She would berate herself and lecture us on not being like her. Once sober, she was quick to point to her errors and turn them into a life lesson as to why it was wrong and why we should never follow her steps.

Mami was very strict. We never were allowed to drink, flirt, or leave her sight. Dating was prohibited, wearing make-up was prohibited. I wasn't allowed to wear make-up until my Junior Prom and then again for my Senior Prom – two special occasions. Doing anything without her being present or without her permission was prohibited. There was no such thing as curfew, as we were always with her.

"I may be a drunk, but I know where my daughters are – where are yours?" she'll proudly proclaim to her critics.

And she was right; we were always under her watchful eyes no matter how much she drank.

Although people called us whores, we were basically really good girls, who would never do anything to shame Mami. Seeing Mami battling with feelings of self-loathing made me protective of her, wanting never to add to her sorrows. Plus, I was superstitious.

The one time I did do something, I was busted! I was in sixth grade and a group of students during recess decided to play spin the bottle. We went to the furthest side of the playground and started to play. Just as luck will have it, our teacher caught us. Oh my God, I was so scared. Was he going to call my mother? He didn't, but that put a big fright in me and a superstition that I wasn't meant to stray too far because with my luck I would be caught.

The superstition was reinforced when some boys were climbing up to our second floor window to play a kissing game with Silvia and Terri. I really wanted to play, but I was so scared. Thus, I just served as the look-out waiting to work up the nerve to participate. Before I did, Eric marched into our room snarling, "Stop that shit!" and walked out. Yup, I wasn't meant to stray. Eric was cool and didn't snitch on us.

Anyway, we were essentially pretty harmless. We knew that Mami was already carrying a huge burden, and we were not going to add to it. Even though I had access to drugs, guys, and drinks, I never engaged in any of this. I have never been drunk in my entire life nor have I ever tried drugs. I was fiercely loyal to Mami; she was my friend.

So while many of the "good girls" would lie to their parents, sneak out, rebel, and soon end up pregnant, drinking, or failing in school, we blossomed academically and never got into trouble. This certainly did not make us popular. Like buzzards over their next meal, many watchful eyes were upon us waiting for the day that we would slip, hoping to gloat. Mami contributed to these antagonistic feelings with her ceaseless boasting of her *nenas* (girls), and we certainly felt the pressure to live up to her high expectations.

Here's another contradiction: some women publicly abhorred her, spoke ill of her, and shunned her. But in private, many sought her counsel and friendship. We had a steady stream of women turning to her for support, and she was genuinely loved by many. She was the "secret" friend. Mami accepted this role, seemingly letting the gossip flow off her back. I, however, saw the damage that others never saw, as she moved from drinking in the weekend, to drinking during the week, to drinking first thing in the morning, a permanent glaze in her big brown eyes.

If my first puppy love experience ended miserably, Silvia's was worst. Unlike me, Silvia is much quieter and conservative, less apt to open up about her feelings, especially her boy interests. One evening when we were out dancing, Silvia caught the eye of a 19-20 year old guy. He was tall, had long brown sandy hair, and was very handsome. We didn't recognize him as a regular to the clubs. He asked Silvia to dance a couple of times and finally worked up the nerve to talk to her. We bumped into him several more times, and it was obvious that he liked her. I could tell that she liked him as well even though she wouldn't say it out loud.

As he started to hang around us more, Mami started flirting with him and dominating the conversations. It put Silvia in an awkward position. Frustrated, Silvia backed off and walked away. Mami was not attuned to Silvia's feelings at all and just continued her flirting, while I inwardly seethed.

Within a couple of days, they became a couple. He never gave Silvia another look. I'm sure Mami thought he was too old for Silvia. As far as she was concerned, he was open game. It was a terrible betrayal. Silvia didn't stand a chance. She could never compete with Mami, but the tragic thing was that she shouldn't have had to.

I was really angry at Mami. It was terribly unfair of her to use her sexuality against Silvia. Silvia was angry as well, but she couldn't say anything. Neither one of us knew how to articulate our feelings out loud, even with each other, without bad mouthing Mami. Therefore, we did what we did best – buried it and build a wall of silence instead of turning to each other for validation and support. This became our family pattern – silence and coping alone.

Besides her unhealthy sexual life and excessive drinking, she also would engage in stealing, an unfortunate family habit. Mami left Bridgeport to get away from some of her family members, but she didn't leave behind this tendency. She wasn't as outrageous as some of her brothers and sisters;

nevertheless, shopping with Mami was an unpleasant experience.

Her favorite thing to do was to change the prices of items. She'll have us be her look-out as she switched the prices on things. At other times, despite our whining and resistance, she'll shove items into our clothes and have us walk out the store, scared to death of being caught. One time, Mami snatched a bra and shoved it into her purse, but she was spotted by a security guard.

"Ma'am, you need to follow me to the security office," said the officer.

My heart sank. We were busted. Mami calmly followed the officer and discreetly discarded the bra into a bin. We all nervously stood crowded in the office. The officer accused her of shoplifting, and she adamantly denied it. They searched her but couldn't find anything.

The officer stepped out and Mami whispered to us, "Oh my God I have a joint on me!" (Mami went through a short marijuana smoking phase).

Thinking quickly she dug out the joint and swallowed it in one gulp. The guard came back and, since he didn't have any evidence, he had no choice but to let us leave with a warning. Relieved, we scrambled out of there, laughing that Mami was going to get a high from the joint in her stomach.

Even a nice country drive to visit Lilly at times included stealing.

"Remember when we would stop by that farm in Mansfield and get our eggs," my husband and his siblings would fondly recall, surprised at the effective honor system that the farmer had of leaving an unattended egg stand for people to help themselves and leave a donation. As I quietly listened, I contrast this conversation with a similar one from my family.

"Remember how we hated when Mami would stop at that egg stand and steal the eggs and donations," we lamented.

A drive to Mansfield also included the day that Mami spotted a 3-speed bicycle in a front yard.

"Look at that bicycle over there. One of you could just go and grab it," she suggested.

"Mami, no" we all groaned.

"Come on. No one is around. Silvia you could do it. See that plaza over there. I'll pull over there and wait for you. Just jump out, grab it and ride it over there," she continued to pressure us as she pulled to a stop.

Feeling coerced, Silvia quickly jumped out of the car, grabbed the bike and started pedaling as fast as she could as Mami pulled away. My heart was pounding as I looked back searching for Silvia.

She pulled up to where we parked and Mami quickly shoved the bike in the trunk and drove away. Mami thought it was hilarious, but none of us thought it was funny as we silently looked at each other feeling horrible that a child was left without a bike! As I said, she was a bag of contradictions.

Mami

Pela de Mosa

WE LIVED IN a time and in an environment where the rod was not spared on children. Comparatively, Mami was the most lenient parent that we knew. She would at times spank us growing up, but as we got older, she started to accumulate our offenses to what she called her *pela de mosa*, the spanking that would initiate us into adulthood. Instead of hitting us, she would simply raise her hand to let us know that another offense had been added.

As I shared before, I was a coward; thus, this threat was enough to snap me into shape. When I was little, five or six years old, I would get a quick whack on the head when Mami, tired of telling all of us to settle down to bed, would come into the bedroom and with a hair brush whack each of us on the head. Only one other time was I slapped. I was 13 years old and was out on our stoop hanging with my cousin, Terri, when I boldly used the "B" word. Quick as a blink, whack, I was slapped on my mouth. Well, that was the end of my swearing days. Fortunately, I never received my *pela de mosa*.

Evi and Silvia, however, were not as lucky. Evi was the first to receive hers. She was 13 years old and was hanging out with a friend that Mami had forbidden her to see. Mami was livid. As she waited for Evi to get home, she thought of how she could best punish Evi. There were two things about Evi that Mami used against her. Evi was extremely modest about her body and hated anyone getting even the slightest glimpse of her body. She was so extremely self-conscious that she even took baths with her underclothes on, which we thought was hilarious. Second, she hated cold water. She would take the hottest showers and come out red as a tomato from her bath.

When Evi finally pranced in the door, Mami lashed out at her in fury. She grabbed her, scolding her along the way, and took her to the bathroom. She stripped her of her clothes and shoved her into a cold shower then proceeded to hit her with a belt. Evi squealed from the cold, the pain, and the utter humiliation as we all watched in shock.

Silvia was the next to receive her *pela de mosa*. Before her big beating, Silvia actually had received a very abusive punishment when she was nine years old. Eric had been teasing Silvia that she had a boyfriend. Silvia would whine and cry that "he's not my boyfriend." The teasing, whining, and crying went on for days. Irritated, Mami decided to punish Silvia for her constant whining. The punishment was that Silvia had to kneel on a grater for a couple of minutes. It drew blood and scarred her knee. As a mother, I find this type of discipline inconceivable.

Nevertheless, this was not the *pela de mosa;* that actually came when Silvia was 16 years old. Mami and Silvia have always bumped heads. Silvia was a headstrong child. She found it hard to apologize or to give in if she felt she was right. Often I would plead with her to just let something go, but she wasn't wired that way and would inevitably end up getting punished. I know this is challenging for a parent as one of my own daughters was the same way. However, instead of trying to break that spunky spirit, I accepted it believing it will serve her well as an adult. Mami, on the other hand, would let it irk her and would engage in a battle of wills.

Mami had called Silvia and asked her to walk Rose over to Mami's friend's apartment on the other side of the projects. Begrudgingly, Silvia walked Rose over and left her in front of the door, not waiting to safely see Rose enter the apartment, but rather rushing back home. Rose, who was around ten years old, took off to play instead of walking into the apartment. When Rose didn't show up, Mami went into a panicked search. When at last she found her, instead of being mad at Rose, Mami was furious at Silvia.

She stormed home in a fury and confronted Silvia, who did not feel it was her fault so she refused to apologize or appear contrite. This made Mami angrier, and the next thing I knew, she grabbed Silvia and slammed her to the floor right into the kitchen steam radiator. Silvia landed on the floor with a loud thump and Mami began to stomp her with her feet, while Silvia just raised her hands to block the blows. Eric and I had to pull Mami away.

Inconceivable!

Trying to Be White

EDUCATION, THANKS TO the grace of my Lord who placed angels in my path to guide me, was my savior and my ticket out of poverty and the projects. I cannot stress enough how important higher education is to breaking the cycle of poverty. I hate to think what my life would have been like if I had chosen a different path. I believe it's a moral imperative to ensure that all of our children are properly educated, that they succeed and finish school, and that they go on to further their education.

My mother only had an eighth grade education and no one in our family had ever graduated high school or attended college. Education was important in the sense that we always had to go to school. There was never any excuse for being absent. However, I don't recall her monitoring our homework, asking about classes, or helping with school work.

Being in the field of education, I constantly hear educators bad mouth parents for not being involved – using it as the number one indicator of bad parenting. Harsh judgment is always cast on those parents who missed an Open House or school event, while those in attendance are treated as the model parents, regardless of what may be the truth behind those families' walls. If only life was truly that simple. My mother never attended an Open House or school event. But she wasn't a bad parent who didn't care about our education. It was just a foreign world where she didn't feel comfortable, especially knowing that she would be judged.

Mami didn't read us bed time stories, yet she still managed to instill a love of reading in me. She collected *novelas*, little Spanish picture-novels featuring the latest actors. She and I would lie on the bed devouring one *novela* after another. Besides *novelas*, we also read *paquitos*, Spanish comic books.

As we lay on her bed reading *novelas*, she would share her stories with me, her dreams, and her disappointments. She called me her *muñeca de cristal*, her crystal doll. She felt I was very dainty, delicate and sensitive. I was the one who would cry reading books, listening to music, or watching television, for which I got mercilessly teased by Eric!

I have to share one of these moments so that you, too, can laugh at me like he loved to do. Visualize me doing dishes. I have pulled a chair to the sink and am washing the dishes sitting down (sounds a little prissy even to me). In the background, *El Trio Los Condes* is singing, *Serenata A Mi Adorada* (Serenade for My Beloved). Now, you must know that I absolutely love old *boleros* from the 50's and 60's – similar to our crooners of the past and present. My favorite Puerto Rican singer is Felipe Rodriquez who played the most poignant songs about lost love, betrayal, and friendships that would deeply stir my soul. Then there were *Los Condes;* how I loved this guitar trio. Their fingers would produce the most incredible magic on the guitar strings. This particular song is about a man who temporarily had to go away from his loved one, but he wrote to her on a daily basis. However, her father, who opposed the relationship, hid the letters. Thinking that she was forgotten and abandoned, she committed suicide. Well, I was so engrossed in the music, the lyrics, and the sounds of the guitars that I was inadvertently crying as I was doing the dishes.

"Boo-hoo, boo-hoo," mimicked Eric who then busted out laughing, and Mami couldn't help to giggle at her *muñeca de cristal*.

Anyway, seeing me as the "sensitive one," Mami called upon me to care for Rose. Rose was deaf from one ear and hearing impaired in the other. She didn't learn to speak until much later in life. For years her verbalization sounded like "gobble, gobble, gobble." Most people didn't have the patience to attempt to understand her or to make the extra effort to communicate in a way that she could understand, specifically speaking loudly and slowly in English, directly facing her and using gestures and facial expressions.

I would get really annoyed when people just assumed that she was mentally retarded and dismissed her. Unfortunately, this happened too often. I sought to include her and Mami would call on me to explain everything to her. While watching television, I was the one that had to sit next to her to explain what was going on. When it was time to explain the facts of life, puberty, and Santa Claus, I was the one that Mami called on.

Seeing me as the nurturing type, mami didn't push high career aspirations in my direction. Those were only directed at Silvia, who was encouraged to be a lawyer or a nurse. For me, she just encouraged me to get married. If I had the need to work, she advised me to work in a bank where I'll get to wear pretty dresses. She also encouraged me to be a secretary as there will always be a need for secretaries, she rationalized. Naturally, I just saw Silvia as the smart one, not me, despite my straight A's and advance courses. I simply assumed that was typical of most students and not really an accomplishment.

Deep down I always knew that Mami was proud of me even though she didn't have high career expectations for me. She would embarrassingly and annoyingly gloat among her peers about me. How studious I was, all the awards I've won, and what a good virgin I was, etcetera, etcetera. Usually this just generated a lot of dislike towards me.

The exception would be when I made the Puerto Rican community as a whole proud. For instance, in my eighth grade graduation and my high school award ceremony I walked away with most of the awards. Then I was embraced by the Puerto Rican community, who clapped, cheered, and showered me in accolades. The rest of the time, however, I was snidely accused of just trying to be white.

Surviving middle school is a challenge for any youth, and I was no exception. Even though there was a "white" middle school around three miles from Charter Oak Terrace, the project kids were bused 15 miles away to a minority school – Quirk Middle School. Quirk had just opened its doors, so unlike my brother and sister who got to attend the good neighboring school, I had the distinct pleasure of being bused straight to a bigger ghetto than Charter Oak Terrace.

Blacks and Puerto Ricans from opposing gangs were all bused into this school. We had the Magnificent 20s, the Ghetto Brothers, and the Savage Nomads all under one roof – wonderful! I lived under the constant threat of Leroy, a leader of the Magnificent 20s, who was killed before he even made it out of high school. He terrorized our halls. He would walk up to any female, including teachers, and fondled their breast or butt. I still recall my Reading Teacher, standing frozen in fear, with tears brimming from her eyes, as he would rub up against her as she stood outside her classroom door. All the girls were petrified of him, but they dealt with his sexual abuse by running, giggling, and screaming. Plus, everyone knew he wouldn't hesitate to punch or hit a girl, having already demonstrated that when he knocked a girl flat with one punch.

I have to believe that I have the greatest guardian angel because I refused to grovel before him and tolerate his abuse, yet he never touched me. I didn't scream, run, or confront him. With clenched fists, where I kept an opened Swiss army knife between my knuckles, I simply looked at him with the coldest stare I could muster. As all the girls scrambled off the chairs and ran away, I would just sit and stare at him, daring him to mess with me. He despised me as much as I despised him.

He looked for any opportunity to harass me. Once, I was writing on the chalk board, and my period seeped through my pants. The teacher tactfully alerted me, and I was excused to the bathroom. Unfortunately, Leroy made it a point to tell everyone what happened and for weeks, whenever I walked by him, he yelled, "Period, Period, Period" pointing at me. Tired of his taunts, I ended up embarrassing him among his friends by sarcastically educating him about menstruation since he was obviously so shocked by it.

After that, he sought to get back at me. He got his chance when I was going to the counselor's office. I was walking with a fellow student when I heard his footsteps behind him. The snickering started, and the usual agitation I felt around him started to creep in. Glancing behind me, I felt myself being stalked like a prey and prickles of apprehension spread. I reached the office relieved to get to my destination, assured that I would be safe now. Unfortunately, instead of the comfort of adult presence, I walked into an empty office; there was no one around.

"Crap, what am I going to do now?"

My walking companion looked at me and took off running leaving me alone in the office with Leroy and his minion, Carl.

Menacingly, he smirked at me, reveling in his power.

"What do you have to say now smart ass," he mocked.

Afraid, I ran behind the office desk to put some distance between us.

"Yeah, you better run skinny bitch. What do you think Carl? We could do her," he taunted.

Looking around, I grabbed a paper weight from the desk, and this deep rage, bubbling inside me, erupted from me. Feeling possessed, I verbally lashed at him with such venom, daring him to touch me, loudly cussing worse than a sailor, doing all that I could to draw attention to my predicament.

"I will kill you m**** f****; I swear, come bring it on!"

Taken aback by the ruckus I was making, he knew he had to leave soon before he got caught. Hastily, he shrugged me off with a "you aren't worth it" and rushed away leaving me standing there with my body trembling out of control as adrenaline coursed through me. I'm sure I must've looked completely insane at that moment. I went on to spend a nightmarish year under his threats.

Thank goodness high school was much better. This time I was bused to Bulkeley High School, which had a large Italian population. The school was just recently integrated so it had a more balance population of Italians, whites, blacks, and Puerto Ricans. At that time, it was considered the best Hartford public school. Our initial welcome to the school was not very positive. The white population was outraged that minorities were being bused into the school. A riot broke out, and I had to seek refuge underneath the cafeteria table, while chairs flew overhead. Mami was so upset at what happened that for the first time ever she kept us home until the fighting subsided. We were in a tough position because we were targeted by both sides since some couldn't tell if we were Puerto Ricans or white.

Besides this eventful start, my high school days were good years for me. I made friends and enjoyed much of high school life, even if I couldn't participate in after school activities as I had to make sure to report back home straight after school. I had many acquaintances but I kept my personal life very private, and I was still teased for "trying to be white."

I most fondly recall our high school prom queen, Erin. She shared homeroom with me for my four years at school yet we were not friends, just mere acquaintances. I really don't know how it even came about, but I must've mentioned that I wasn't attending prom because I didn't have anything to wear. And this girl, whom I barely knew, very graciously lent me her junior prom dress. I was so touched by this very kind gesture that allowed me to enjoy my senior prom.

Another major highlight was when I was declared student of the month. As I shared earlier, I never considered myself smart despite my excellent grades. Consequently, when I won this honor from among many Hartford students, I felt very special, and it helped to boost my self-confidence. The honor culminated with a special dinner for the nine recipients of the year and their families. This was the very first time I ever attended a formal dinner. Dining out for us was limited to *Aqui Me Quedo*, the local Puerto Rican restaurant, or if we were being fancy, Ponderosa.

Mami and Silvia attended the dinner with me. We were all nervous as we faced all the utensils in front of us. Mami whispered, "just copy what everybody else does."

We happily survived the dinner without any major mishap. It's funny how these little events can deeply touch a person and why it's so important to offer such types of affirming programs.

Sleepless Nights

I LAY TOSSING and turning, trying not to disturb Silvia who shared the full-size bed with me. I'm on high alert, listening to every noise, waiting for Mami to get home. I finally hear the door downstairs. Fully awake, I strain to hear every nuance, trying to get a sense if they arrived happy, angry, drunk, playful. Soon, Mami and Miguel stumble up the stairs, slightly inebriated as usual.

When they finally go into their bedroom and close their door, I make my move. I quietly sneak out of my bed, careful not to wake up Silvia. I crack the door, hoping it doesn't creak, taking my time. I tiptoe out, and gently close the bedroom door. Silvia is fast asleep, not noticing my departure. Eric and Rose's door is closed, so I move silently across the hall until I'm right outside Mami's door.

I stop and put my ear on the door and began to listen, not knowing if tonight there will be an argument or would they go off to sleep. I crouch down, and take my position outside the door, leaning back on the door with my ear directly on the door so that I could best hear the sounds from within. I hear muffled voices. A moan – but is that a sexual noise or not? At twelve years old, I'm not quite sure. So I listen harder – is she okay? Oh no, voices are starting to escalate – an argument ensues. This goes on – will they stop and go off to sleep? I wait.

Then I hear the first sounds of a struggle – a scuffle – that's my cue. I jump up and run to Silvia. I gently shake her shoulder, "wake up, they're fighting."

Silvia jumps up and runs to Mami's aide, while I run to Eric and wake him up as well. I leave Rose sleeping. With her hearing impairment, she is sheltered from this drama and sleeps right through it. The troop is ready. Silvia goes straight for Miguel's neck, jumping on his back. At 14, she's short – 4 feet 10 inches and she's thin, weighing no more than 90 pounds. But she's quick, determined, and strong. She latches on to his back and pummels his back with her little fists. Eric runs to Mami and secures her in a bear hug as she tries to get away, clawing, swearing, and kicking.

I'm down to my last move, I run to the phone and call the cops, "Hurry, there's a fight."

Silvia is fighting Miguel, Eric is trying to talk sense into Mami, and I run to Miguel to begin talking to him – I usually could calm him down.

"Miguel, please stop. Calm down. I called the police; they're on their way. Please stop," I plead with him.

Tempers are still flying when I hear the police pounding on our door. I rush downstairs to let them take over. Silvia, stoic as usual, stands to the side, glaring at Miguel. She's not a screamer or a crier. She takes his hits but does not give him the pleasure of knowing that he hurt her. Instead, she smirks at him and gives a deadly, triumphant stare. You can't hurt

Mami, we're all here and we'll stop you. Eric stays with Mami calming her down, while I talk to the police – rational and responsible. This scene is one that repeated itself over and over.

We each had our role to keep Mami safe. How and why we fell to these roles, I don't know. Part of me believes that relegating Eric to attending to Mami was a way of protecting him. At 15, a martial arts student, the last thing we needed was Eric getting into a serious fight with Miguel and landing in jail. It was just safer to have him control Mami. Therefore, Silvia was the one who would have to take the hits and worse, have to live under the constant threats of Miguel.

Miguel liked me and ironically was the one that started me in my desire to write by presenting me a journal that I kept until I was married. I didn't approve of him, but I knew he was over his head and that he needed to walk away from this unhealthy relationship with Mami.

He avoided Eric. Eric never says much, but he's intimidating. You know that he won't waste words, and he could easily have hurt Miguel. Miguel kept a wide berth from him. Silvia, however, was another story. She was his nemesis, the one that took him directly on.

Mind you, Miguel was just an insecure 20 year old playing grown up with a 34-year old woman. The only way he thought he could control her was through violence. Between us watching over her and Mami's own feistiness, she never really got hurt. He's the one that always ended up in the losing side, so his wrath was directed at Silvia. She lived under the constant threat that he was going to get her one day.

Silvia and I would sit in the stoop of our back door, watching life around us. Miguel would saunter behind her, sharpening his machete making up menacing songs: "I'm watching you. Yes, I am. When you least expect it, swish, there goes your head."

She would look at me, rolling her eyes, bravely showing no fear as if he couldn't rattle her. Yes, we knew we could easily beat him up, but he still was scary. He was unpredictable and obsessed with Mami, a volcano waiting to erupt.

The thought of something happening to Mami, whether because of Miguel or her drinking, resulted in my inability to sleep through the nights. I was always on high alert, ready to react to any commotion that may ensue, sleeping with one eye open. Sleepless nights were a reasonable price to pay to keep Mami safe, except when she finally needed me the most, and I slept through the night, both eyes firmly shut.

Angels

THE DRAMA THAT Miguel brought into our house was endless nights of fights and police visits. One night, one of the police officers noticed me. He saw me trying to keep it together, being the family spokesperson, being responsible.

He pulled me to the side, and he said the most powerful words that anyone could have ever said to me, "You know, life does not have to be this way."

Wow – that was a powerful statement. Violence and chaos were all that I knew. It surrounded my whole life and the life of everyone around me. Long after he left, those words entered my soul and fed a fire in me. He would never know the long-lasting impact he had on my life. Life does not have to be this way.

Inadvertently, the policeman planted a seed in me, a seed that grew into a burning desire to get out. This is why I tell people that you never know when you make a difference in someone's life; you just have to do your work on blind faith that it will. I truly believe this officer was an angel placed in my path to point me in a new direction. I had no idea how I would get out, but all I knew was that I must get out. I wanted out of the projects and the life that I've always known. I was never one to dream. I just had one goal – to get out.

When teachers or adults asked, "so what do you want to do when you grow up?" I just wanted to scream in their face, "What the F**** do I know – I just want OUT, OUT, OUT!" But, of course, I just smiled and shrugged.

I was so lost. There wasn't a clear path for me. Silvia had been prepped for college her whole life. She was the first to graduate high school. I was so proud of her accomplishment. She had dreams and direction as she went off to become a nurse.

Regrettably, this road quickly ended because she was thrown ill-prepared to a foreign world where she was the only non-white student at her small, elite college. She had earned a four-year scholarship due to her outstanding grades. As part of the scholarship, she had a different lunch pass than the other students, marking her as being there on scholarship. Instead of taking pride in this accomplishment, she felt ashamed.

The other students treated her as an affirmative action charity case and avoided her, not being rude, but also not being inclusive – just polite. Silvia, who always hated attention, now felt like she stuck out like a sore thumb and didn't fit in. Something as simple as taking care of her hair brought unnecessary negative attention to her.

Puerto Ricans are very familiar with the hair routine. First, you had to put your hair up in large curlers, wait all day for them to dry, and then sleep with a *doobie*. A *doobie* entailed putting a large curler on the center of your head, then wrapping your hair around the curler to do the final straightening of the hair. You can imagine what this looked like to those who had never seen this, and she felt horribly self-conscious.

Her sense of isolation grew and grew until she finally decided to quit. Still desperately wanting out of the projects, she did the next best thing – she fell in love and married. Unfortunately, she married a drug addict and a thief. A man, yet again, busted another dream.

Evi had long ago run-away from home soon after we moved to Hartford. It wasn't until I was an adult that I could begin to understand her story a little better. As a child, all I knew was that Evi ran away and turned her back on my mother. Mami was very bitter and angry at her, and, being fiercely loyal to Mami, I simply accepted the anger from Mami's perspective. She became stricter with Silvia and me, again Evi's fault.

But how does a 13 year old truly decides to run away with a 27 year old man? She doesn't. The truth is that she was manipulated by a rapist, a child molester who absconded with her to Puerto Rico and used her. It's just rape, and it's sick.

What really happened is that William had been showering Evi with attention. Flattered, she was tricked into going with him to a motel where he had intercourse with her. Evi recalls being scared and confused, not knowing how to stop it or what was going on. She was in so much pain that she limped for two days. Afraid of Mami's reaction, she didn't tell Mami what happen. William then reappeared at her school and told her he was picking her up to take her home. Evi went with him, but instead of going home, he took off with her. Before she even knew what was going on, she was in Puerto Rico with this man who used her for his sexual pleasure and then abandoned her with his mother. By the time she made it back to America, Mami had washed her hands of Evi and never sought her side of the story.

Poor Evi was thrown into a life of exploitation and violence before she even knew what hit her. She went from one horrific relationship to another, violence always nipping at her door. I remember when she lived with this horrible man, another William, who would beat her terribly. One day she called for help. Mami, Silvia and I rushed to her side. We found her chained to the bedpost, on the floor, like a dog.

Oh, how I was growing to despise men and now Silvia appeared to be going down the same path. I vowed never to fall in love. I was already reserved, so it was easy to build a bigger, stronger wall. I would not allow myself to have illusions. The biggest mistake a man could do was to buy me a flower or to try to woo me. The cynic in me would leap forward, questioning what the hell he wanted.

I did end up having a boyfriend, Pablito, throughout most of my high school years. He played baseball for the league we always supported so my private wall did not have to be penetrated as he already knew us. One day after the game, he was talking to me at the Domino's Club. In his uniform, I always assumed he was just another adult. When he shared that he was 15 years old like me, I was taken aback. Here I was being myself, not shy and awkward, thinking he was just one of the other older men and all of a sudden he was a peer, and one that actually liked me. I was clueless and never noticed. We sat in the fire escape getting more acquainted, and he asked me out the next day. I told him he would have to come by my house and ask Mami's permission.

I've never seen him out of uniform so when he came by looking like a 15 year-old, dressed up to make a good impression, I found myself feeling a little shy. It was very sweet, and he instantly won Mami's favor and blessings. Soon we grew into a serious couple. He was very devoted to me and to my family, and he fitted right into our lifestyle.

Mami loved him; she could just hear those wedding bells she desperately wanted for me. In my senior year, he proposed to me in the kitchen right in front of Mami. Surprised and a bit self-conscious, I was content to get engaged. Nevertheless, uneasiness dwelled in me.

As wonderful as he was, he was from my world. His family had drama, drank, and many detested Mami and me – same-o, same-o. I loved him and he loved me, but I didn't have the confidence that marriage with him would truly be my ticket out. Deep down I was too afraid to even give him a chance.

The pressure of taking care of Mami was mounting. I knew I would have to take care of her, and I was willing to do that, but when would I be ready to assume that role?

She had left Miguel, but continued her philandering and drinking. With Silvia gone and me in a relationship, Mami found a new circle of friends to go dancing and drinking with. Without us always by her side, her drinking escalated. In place of the dance clubs, she now lived in the bars, a male-dominated environment for more hard-core drinking. Breakfast became gin and milk or a beer, accompanied by a story of how she hit a roll of parked cars driving home.

I worried. I could see her fear of being alone mounting. I shared her fear. What was going to happen to her? Rose worried. Unable to articulate her concerns, she resorted to watering down Mami's beer. Oh boy, did she almost get her *pela de mosa* for that one. We didn't know quite what to do or say.

One incident, which is going to sound really harsh on my part, also made me feel as she was deteriorating even faster. After a night out, she came to see me all giddy waiting to share her latest exploits.

"I was wrong. I was completely wrong. White men are not cold fish," she exclaimed.

She had her first sexual encounter with a white man. I was speechless. I didn't even know how to respond. This was terribly wrong of me, but I felt like she had crossed all boundaries. She hit bottom. Anything was possible now.

My graduation was growing nearer, and I was no clearer to knowing what I was going to do. I had applied and won numerous scholarships, but I didn't quite know what to do with them. But, our Lord is so powerful, that He put another angel in my path. Following Silvia's footsteps, I had been involved in Upward Bound, a program for first generation college bound students. The Director, Mr. Guzman, was totally disgusted with me. He saw me wasting my brains, being engaged at 17 years old, applying to community colleges in Rhode Island, with no clue of what to do.

He called me to his office and confronted me, "What are you doing?"

"I don't know – I just want out. I want to go away as far as I can. I don't care what I study. I just want out."

Thankfully he took over. He picked my college for me, completed the application and made all the arrangements for me to go away. He felt that I, who never had been outside of the projects, should not wander off to a new state. Therefore, he put me under the care of a friend. I had my ticket out, and I ran as fast as I could, never looking back.

Culture Shock

I WAS PACKED and ready to go, excited and scared at the same time. Central Connecticut State College, which subsequently became Central Connecticut State University (CCSU), was located in New Britain, a small city approximately fifteen miles from Charter Oak Terrace. The drive was a pretty drive through the suburbs of West Hartford and Farmington. Outside of Hartford, you could see the large maple and oak trees, famous for the beautiful Connecticut foliage. Additionally, the landscape consisted of great rolling hills, especially in New Britain. The campus was on the outskirts of the city, near a beautiful tree-lined residential area.

Mami drove up the steep hill to my assigned dorm, located in a quad of four large, brick residential buildings. My assigned room was in Gallaudet Hall on the second floor. With few belongings to cart to my room, Mami didn't even get out of the car. She hastily said her good-byes and drove away without ever seeing my room. Being out of her element was very uncomfortable for her. She didn't attend the parent's orientation nor did she take me to my orientation. I had to make my own travel arrangements and go on my own.

For a 17 year-old, I thought I was wise and grown. After all, I knew about life, about good and evil. I was grounded in solid values. Yes, I was ready for this new world as I faced a new chapter of my life with no rose color glasses.

I grew up in a time where there was no cable television, just three to four channels; there was no internet, and all I knew was how to survive the ghetto. I had no knowledge about the greater world around me – just stereotypes. If there were stereotypes against Puerto Ricans, we had our full share of stereotypes about white people. First, they were all smart. The first thing I warned Mami was not to be disappointed if I no longer brought straight As home. After all, I was now entering a white world, where everyone would surely be smarter than me. Second, I teased, at least she didn't have to worry about my virginity. We knew white men were cold fishes. Despite her one experience to the contrary, I chose to deny that one incident ever occurred. Third, what was I going to do with myself? I was going to be terribly bored since white people didn't party. We knew they were like the Brady Bunch, perfect people with no drama in their life. Yes, I thought I was prepared for this new world. Not!

There was a whole world out there that I knew nothing about, and I experienced a complete culture shock. I've led a pretty insular life with no exposure to the greater community. Something as simple as breakfast became foreign. I remember my first breakfast. I grabbed a spoonful of oatmeal, ready to savor the rich creamy sweetness, only to find myself gagging. What is this? It wasn't rich, smooth, or sweet – it was a watery, bland, gooey substance. I didn't know I had to add my own brown sugar and doctor it up. And let's not talk about the coffee. There was no description; I had to quickly spit out what tasted to me like a cup of hot water with a tinge of coffee. Needless to say, that beyond the school lunches, I had not been exposed to American cuisine. Believe me, I adjusted and broadened my horizon, and the best thing was that I enjoyed having three full-meals a day. In my four years of college, I never missed a meal. Those days of being hungry were gone!

Then came the change in music and popular culture. Me, the dance queen who knew every Latin artist and genre, now was immersed in English music that I never heard of – could you even dance to this? I remember the day that John Lennon was shot. Tremendous sorrow and shock spread through the campus, and I just sat there wondering, "who is he?" I had no idea. My exposure to English music was limited to what I saw on television, some Beatles, Jackson Five, and Elvis. I didn't realize John Lennon was a Beatle.

The biggest shock of all was to see that some white people were wild – many even more wild than Puerto Ricans. The drinking and sex around me was scandalous. I have never witnessed such behavior. Although Mami may have been an alcoholic and free with her sexual favors, this was way different, at an entirely new level. Mami's behavior was shameful and not to be celebrated – she was an outcast to be criticized and judged. When she drank, she was a quiet drunk and not a loud, wild drunk who joked about it the next day as if it was totally acceptable. We didn't discuss Mami's drinking – it was a taboo subject, and we mastered the art of denial.

In contrast, on campus, drinking and sex were as accepted as apple pie for dessert. There was no trying to save your virginity for marriage. The shame, disappointment, and judgment when someone did lose their virginity didn't exist in this world. Sex was expected and normal.

Contrary to my high school days, I now sought security and connection in the small Puerto Rican/Latino community that existed on campus. They became a haven. Now I understood why Mr. Guzman didn't want me to leave so far to another state. I had no exposure to the outside world and was not well prepared.

In fact, college gave me my first exposure to: bowling, roller skating, American theaters, trips to New York, Boston, canoeing, vacations, and museums – just doing anything outside a five-mile radius from the projects. I loved it. I was studying and still getting my As while having fun with normal people. No more fights or drama. My own internalized stereotypes were mercifully crumbling, seeing the strength, beauty, and diversity of my fellow Puerto Ricans and white counterparts.

Like Silvia, I had to deal with being a minority on campus and with a few students who resented our presence, assuming we didn't earn the right to be there. We had to put up with heckling and sneers.

"Hey, are you ready? Okay, I'll be up in a second."

Vivian and I walked down her hall. As we passed an open door of her fellow floor mates, four guys saw us and came out of their room and began to follow us.

"*Andale, Andale*," they mocked, using a cliché Mexican insult.

Quickening our pace, we rushed to the elevator trying to get away from their derision.

Furthermore, it was my routine to study every day in the library because the dorms were too loud. Music was always playing in the background, coupled with the usual noise of young adults having a good time. I understood, so I simply went to the quieter environment that I preferred.

Ironically, however, the same tolerance was not reciprocated. On the extremely rare occasions that my friends and I gathered in the lounge, we would be quickly disbanded or reprimanded for making too much noise. Previously ignored rules would now be strictly enforced.

A group of minorities together was threatening; we had to integrate fast, acculturate, and become less visible. It was okay for like-minded individuals to be drawn together – athletes, thespians, fraternities – as long as the group that came together was not based on race. I say specifically race, because it was also okay for the Italian Club, International Club, and other ethnic groups to sit together. It was the visible minority that was unacceptable.

Frustrated by this treatment, I wrote an editorial to the paper. I didn't mean to cause a commotion, but the next thing I knew my academic record was being pulled, "Who is this troublemaker?"

I'm only aware of this because I knew staff who worked in the Dean's office, and they shared what a frenzy I inadvertently caused. When my record was pulled, and they saw that I was an outstanding student, then I became credible. I was called into meetings to address the treatment of minority students on campus, was assigned to a committee to address the concerns of minority students, and soon was awarded a Presidential Citation for my leadership on minority affairs on campus.

Regardless of these types of cultural adjustments, college was a sanctuary for me. There were many great and diverse people that were enlarging my narrow view of the world. Charter Oak was a nice distant past. The best part was that I learned to sleep through the night without being on alert, listening for fights, break-ins, or waiting for Mami to get home safely. What a refreshing treat.

Glass of Milk

DURING MY FIRST semester, I ended up breaking my engagement to Pablito. He was away in the army while I was in college. He was a great man, but he came from my world. I realized how sheltered I'd been, and I wanted to start experiencing the positive parts of life. There was a new potential love interest (turned out to be my future husband) that I wanted to explore.

Nonetheless, I wasn't going to make that decision lightly. I made my list – because love and romance was never going to rule me. Poor Pablito had too many strikes against him. He drank, he had drama in his family, he was from the projects – I just saw a world that was too familiar to me – too negative. I felt horrible for breaking his heart and Mami's heart as well, but I broke the engagement. I didn't want to take a risk. It turned out that he too broke out of the projects and did well for himself, but I was to scare to even take a chance of being stuck there.

"So now you think you're white, too good for us," Mami badgered me.

Part of her anger was due to an incident that happened before I left to college. Before college started, Pablito and I discussed whether we should have sex before we parted ways. We were engaged, in love, so why not? I wrote a letter to Mami asking permission. I left it for her to find while I was in school. I wrote all my arguments as to why I thought it was a good idea.

"Oh boy, what have I done? Is she going to be mad at me?" I wondered as I nervously glanced at the clock in the classroom waiting for dismissal.

I came home and with my head down. I hesitantly walked in not knowing what to expect. She didn't say a word so I went into my bedroom where I found a note on my bed. In the letter, she eloquently delineated her arguments as to why she thought it was a bad idea for me to have premarital sex. Despite, her argument, she finished the letter by granting me permission since I had taken the risk to ask her opinion.

I called Pablito and told him I decided against having sex. If I could give her the "getting married as a virgin" dream I was going to try, plus she had good arguments about why I shouldn't. Because of this incident, she now was really confused by my current actions. I really couldn't explain it to her. How could I tell her how badly I wanted out of the projects, her home, and the life she had given me? I really just wanted the time to explore and discover a new world, but it wasn't her world. I couldn't explain this. I accepted her disappointment until she moved on and accepted my decision.

Going home was always difficult. There never was anyone able or willing to bring me back to campus. I felt like a burden, and I would be resentful and angry that I had to resort to taking a bus back to campus. Mami would promise that someone would bring me back, but then when it was time, I would have to tote my overnight bag to the bus stop, transfer to another bus just to make it back to campus. In retrospect, I can't really complain since this is how I met Frank, my husband. I knew him from campus but not very well. As I stood at the bus stop, he and his brothers saw me and offered me a ride. This started our friendship and our eventual romance, so who am I to question life's inconveniences? Nevertheless, I started avoiding going home so as not to deal with the hassle of getting back to campus.

But summer was here, and I was back home for at least a couple of weeks until my summer job on campus started. The first morning, I woke up to find that Mami was already up. She had made me breakfast and packed me a lunch for my temporary job in the tobacco fields. You have to understand, this rarely happened. We always did our own breakfast. On the weekend, she sometimes would put a pot of coffee on the stairs. The rich aroma of coffee would drift up the stairs and like the Pied Piper's music, we all would be drawn out of our room and down the stairs. However, getting up early on a weekday to have breakfast and lunch waiting for me was definitely an anomaly. She wanted me to meet the new and improved Elisa.

"Look at me – I'm a *señora* now" – a proper lady, settled down with her man, as she awkwardly smiled at me.

I stared in shock. She had aged since I was gone. She was jittery and insecure, seeking my approval. Where was the voracious, spitfire 41-year old woman that I knew and loved? This was not her. My heart broke. She knew I could see right through her and the farce of the relationship that she was currently in.

Yes, she was settled with one man, Chely, playing housewife to an abhorrent bully. Her beautiful smile now featured a toothless gap, which I later found out he knocked right out with a punch. This was no Miguel that Mami could easily over-power and control. Miguel was young, skinny and lanky. Mami never feared or was injured by Miguel. His attempts to control her elicited laughter, not fear, in her. Now for the first time ever, I saw real fear in Mami.

Chely was in his late forties. He was around 5'8" and a solid mass of muscle. He easily weighed around 200 pounds. He was that one softball player that would hit the big homeruns, the power hitter.

He never raised his voice; there was never any scene in the house, on the surface a soft spoken gentleman. Underneath this projected image dwelled the heart of a tyrant waiting to strike and assert control.

"Mami, what happened," I inquired looking at her black eye, something I have never seen on my mother.

"Oh, it's nothing."

"What do you mean nothing? Is Chely hitting you?"

"*Nena*, don't get upset. He didn't mean to. You know how I am. He doesn't like when other men look at me. He's a good man; he loves me. He promised me he won't ever do it again."

"I didn't hear you guys fighting. When did this happen?"

"In the car as we were driving back. He's really embarrassed and afraid of seeing you."

"Well he should be!"

"Please, please don't get mad. Now that your home he'll stop. He really feels bad."

"I don't give a crap how he feels. Why are you still with him? You have to stop this."

"Ma-ma, I'm getting old. I have to settle down. I don't want to be alone. You don't want me alone either, do you? It'll get better; you'll see."

"Mami, that's nonsense. I rather you be alone than getting abused."

"You don't understand. Please for me, don't get into it with him. Trust me. He'll stop. Look at me, I'm better now. I'm not drinking as much, hanging in the bars. I'm trying to be a *señora*."

Much as she tried, I was very upset. She's never been hurt by a man before. Rose confirmed to me that this was not the first time. Chely would wait until he was alone with her, trapped in the car, then he would punch her and let her have it. Rose said she'll come home with a black eye or busted lip, with serious injuries in her face. Mami, who always spoke against domestic violence, who instilled strong pride in her girls not to ever take any man's shit, was a battered woman, trapped and afraid and making excuses for his behavior.

That evening as I lay on my bed, Chely finally had the nerve to come home.

"Can I come in?" he asked, peeking his head in my room.

I didn't respond, giving him a dirty look instead.

"Don't be mad at me," he said as he entered the room and kneeled down next to my bed.

"I'm really sorry. You have no idea how much I love your mother. I didn't mean to hurt her. I promise I'll never do that again," crying he pleaded his case before me.

Sniveling fool! What audacity to come crying to me, seeking my forgiveness.

"Believe me. She's so mad at me. She really wants us to get along. For her, please forgive me. I'll never hit her again. You'll see. She means the world to me."

Tired of my silent stare, he gave up and walked away. I couldn't utter a single word. Expressing my anger is not natural for me, so all I could do was muster a contemptuous face and project my disgust.

As always, this episode had to be relegated to a deep abyss where all emotions were stored. Exhausted and disappointed, summer was finally coming to an end, and I was ready to retreat back to my sanctuary, relieved that I didn't have to look at him anymore nor look at this new Mami playing the domestic role.

I was packed and ready to go. It was a Sunday morning, August 29th when the house of cards came falling down.

The house was quiet; I was the first to wake up after sleeping through the night. Heading to the bathroom, I saw that Mami's door was ajar. It usually was closed. Did she not come home last night?

I glanced in, and there was Mami lying face down on the floor, with just her underwear. Maybe because of my tendency to expect the worse, I instinctively knew that she was dead. I didn't run in but rather I walked in and kneeled beside her. I reached to touch her and found her cold to my touch.

I looked around and Chely was nowhere to be found, instead there was an unknown brown mutt in the bedroom. Mind you, Mami was allergic to dogs and never cared for them. Now there was one sitting right there in the bedroom with her, with his tongue hanging, quiet as a mouse staring at me. He didn't even stir when I entered the room.

I felt a calm overtake me, mirroring the same stillness the dog was projecting, numbing myself to the scene before me.

I got up and woke up Rose and sent her to our neighbors with the dog. I called the police and my sisters and went back to kneel by Mami's side. I stared at her body, but I didn't see Mami. I saw a shell, a body without a soul. Mami's spirit was gone.

Bowing my head, I prayed.

"Dear God, thank you. Thank you for taking her from this living hell. She was so tired and didn't deserve this. Thank you, Lord. Please give her peace. She has suffered so much, please give her rest. Dear Lord, please have mercy. She surely has paid for all her sins; please take her into Your loving arms and reunite her with *papi que se murio, abuela,* and all her loved ones."

I prayed and prayed without a tear in my eye, just this tremendous sense of relief, relief that it was over. All I saw for her was a future filled with more pain and loneliness. I didn't know where it was going to end. Fervently, I wished I could have made things better for her but I couldn't. I couldn't protect her. In fact, the one night that she needed me the most, I failed her and slept through the night. The irony of that didn't escape me.

I closed my eyes. Images of her having an asthma attack, gasping for breath, trying to find her inhaler came to mind. But no one was there to help her, to fan her, to find her spray – she was utterly alone, her greatest fear had come to life.

Subsequently, I found out that Chely's constant threat to Mami was that he was going to hide her inhaler on her. It appeared that he followed through on those threats.

For a second, I felt a tinge of bitterness wanting to crawl into my soul, "I'm glad You finally took her, but did she have to die this way? Alone, helpless, scared, gasping for breath! God, that is so unfair."

But, I had to shake those images away or they would consume me. I blocked those thoughts and focused on the good. It was over for her. She'll be with Jesus. Yes, these were better images. She was going to be okay – I knew this deep in my soul, this sense of absolute certainty that she was better off. Thank you Lord. Thank you Lord.

Soon I was drawn back to reality as everyone started arriving. Elizabeth, the caretaker, was back on duty. It was easier this way and better than letting emotions get the best of me. I tended to my sisters and called my brother, who had just gotten married that same week. Not the best honeymoon, that's for sure; he quickly arranged to come home. I then called the extended family, made all the funeral arrangements, and focused on details.

Before her wake, I asked for my own private time with her. I had selected a grey dress that I had bought her on Mother's Day. The dress had a string belt that ended in a small knot that formed into a soft ball. Mami loved softness. Whenever she found anything soft, she would use it to trace a circle on my palms. It was her form of endearment. I broke off the ball and lovingly tucked it into her folded hands so she would eternally have this soft remembrance of me in her hand.

For years a favorite pastime of mine was putting make-up on Mami. I would dive into her bed and beg her to let me make her up. She had the smallest lips. I would enjoy putting all different types of shades on them, experimenting with various looks. For her eyes, I would practice shading techniques in the crevice of the eye to create depth. She had little eyebrows; they were thin and short. Thus, I would darken them with eyebrow pencil, thereby covering her scar from the car accident. After applying her make-up, I would do body art on her, using her body as my art canvas. She always patiently tolerated my game, basking in the love I showered on her.

Now as we approached our last moments together, I wanted to personally do her hair and her make-up one last time. I went in early and gently combed her hair and made her as beautiful as I could for her last public appearance. I sat alone with her, saying my good-bye, pouring my love with every stroke of the brush.

Mami's last picture with the dress she was buried in.

Fearing that any display of support would make me cry, I asked my friend Carmen to please keep everyone away from me. I didn't want to cry or fall apart. The wake and funeral were packed. Mami was well-known, and although sometimes disapproved of, she was equally loved. The funeral parlor was filled to capacity, standing room only. There were many faces from our past and present there, showing their support and love for my mother. Carmen did a great job keeping everyone away from me, and I was able to remain calm, focused, and in control.

I did such a good job hiding my emotions that I even had an idiot come up to me and comment, "Oh, I guess you weren't that close to her." What a fool – I just looked at her and walked away. Mami and I knew better. We knew what we shared.

Eric, however, could see through the façade, and he was determined to crack through it. After years of teasing me for crying while watching television, I now couldn't cry, and he sought to get me to cry. It was time for the funeral procession to the cemetery, which was in Bridgeport, a good one hour drive.

One of Mami's ex-lovers didn't know how to get there. I agreed to ride with him. Looking back now, I could see how hard I was working at taking care of others in order to avoid my own feelings. Weird as it was, I rode with him instead of my family. When Mami was with him, I resented him because he was married, and here I now sat with him for the long drive. I witnessed his genuine grief as he openly cried and shared with me how much he loved Mami. In an unexpected role reversal, I listened and comforted him during the drive.

Once at the cemetery, Eric quickly reappeared by my side, wanting me to know he was there for me.

"He's worried about me," I thought.

As if I was out of my body looking in, I saw my concerned brother hovering around me. I made a conscious decision to just let him have that, let him comfort me, let him be my big brother and support me. When everyone departed, I let the weight that had been on my shoulder envelop me and I collapsed and cried in his arms.

I then packed my emotions back in and finished with all the remaining arrangements and decisions. What happens to Rose? For years I was the closest to her. I knew she wanted me to take care of her. But how could I? Do I quit college, keep the apartment, and take care of her? I wish I could tell you I was that magnanimous – I wasn't. Eric was the best logical choice. At least we can take Rose away from the projects to a new state, I rationalized. We could get her out. I felt guilty for many years for letting Rose down at a time she really needed me, second guessing myself and my decisions. Forevermore, Rose was left with a deep scar from this decision, feeling rejected by her family, never understanding that we, too, were lost children trying to survive.

Then the decision came as to what to do with the apartment. I advocated that we let Evi have it. She was the neediest at that time as a single mother. Finally, I was ready to return to campus, where the tears finally came at the most inopportune times and in spurts, but they moved me towards the road to recovery.

What an eye opener this was for me. I really had no one to call, to lean on, or to share with. A side effect of living with chaos and alcoholism was that we each coped privately and independently, a result of denial. To call on my siblings felt like I would be burdening them. Thus, here I was 18 years old and I really didn't have a single true friend in the world.

My one friendship with Carmen abruptly ended. Our relationship was already strained once I left for college. She had written to me obsessing about a married man that she was interested in. She was contemplating having sex with him in the hopes of getting pregnant and forcing him to stay with her. She was writing her confused thoughts, thoughts of a young girl who craved love. Practical me wrote back advising her against this relationship, but if she insisted in having sexual relations that the least she should do was get birth control. I offered to help her if she chose that path.

Unfortunately, this letter was intercepted by her mother who became outraged. She didn't want anything else to do with me and didn't want me near Carmen again. I was resentful that Carmen didn't defend me, allowing her mother to think I was advocating sex. Obviously Carmen was in a predicament and couldn't reveal the complete story; but, nevertheless, I was hurt that my only friendship in Charter

Oak, this particular family, had vilified me and turned their back on me.

That summer, our friendship was already fragile. Then when Mami died, and I asked her to keep everyone away from me, she was the only one physically near me and this was the moment she chose to "come-out" to me by attempting to kiss me. I was stunned at the incredible bad timing and just didn't want to deal with it right then.

Before I could attempt to reach out to her, news reached me that she started living with my aunt. Her mother was outraged and again blamed me, casting me as the villain for "encouraging her to homosexuality." What could I say? I just didn't want to deal with this. Mami's body was barely underground, and this new drama erupted. Avoidance was just easier. There was never any closure, and I do regret that she was left with the impression that our friendship broke up because of her pass to me. It was not the case at all. The timing sucked, and I needed the space to grieve and heal.

Now I was all alone with my grief. Even though I had broken up with Pablito, if he had just picked up the phone, I probably would had given everything up and flown away and married him on the spot. But, God knows what He does, so instead I stood alone. Mami, my dearest friend, was gone, and I had no one else to fill that spot. Something was terribly wrong with this picture, and I never ever wanted to be in this lonely place again.

Mami's words of wisdom held me strong: *"no te ahogues en un vaso de leche,"* don't drown in a glass of milk. Yes, survival – that I knew. It was time to buck up and rebuild, which meant it was time for me to change. No more private, shy Elizabeth. I knew that I had to put myself out and make real friends, not just mere acquaintances. Determined, I formed stronger, more meaningful friendships that I still maintain today.

However, I was essentially homeless. Campus was home but during the breaks I needed to make arrangements for myself. Initially, I turned back to my old room and stayed with Evi.

One evening I was sleeping in my old room when all of a sudden, I felt a soft caress on my calf. I opened my eyes and this dark face was hovering inches from my face, breathing hard and smelling my hair.

"Ahhhh, Ahhhh!!!" I jerked up, kicking and letting out the loudest bloodcurdling scream. His fingernail cut into my leg, and surprised by my screams, he ran down the stairs and out the door.

"What, what," Evi rushed into the room.

"A man, a man," I barely blurted out and continued my ceaseless screaming for a good ten minutes straight, long after he was gone, waking up the entire neighborhood.

When the policeman arrived, he found the knife that the intruder used to break through the screen of the downstairs window. By the grace of God, the intruder had left the knife downstairs. I shivered at the thought of what would have happened if he had carried the knife with him into my room. Then to top it all off the police offered me the knife as a souvenir. The nerve!

I felt physically sick, quaking in fear and rage, feeling violated yet incredibly grateful to God that I wasn't raped. This was the last straw. I couldn't do this anymore. I didn't have the stamina or desire to continue with anything remotely related to my past. Although Evi and Silvia would always have a room for me, for all intents and purposes, I was homeless. I had to make it on my own.

For the next three years, I lived on campus, including the summers when I worked as a Camp Counselor. During the times that the campus closed and was inaccessible to me, I bounced between my friends' homes. Like my turtle kindred spirit who carries its home on its back, I made do, surviving as best I could.

Me one month before Mami died

Blessings

"MAMI, REMEMBER THIS picture. This is when Elyssa told the man, "flip me, flip me" and instead he pushed her down the zip line not understanding a word of English," Raquel laughs and everyone's joins in drawing me out of my reverie.

"Get the video," Elyssa suggests and now everyone moves to the living room for our favorite pass-time: home movies.

Life has changed so drastically for me. I find myself surrounded by a huge, loving, close-knit family filled with incredible memories of laughter and adventure. A simple birthday party with just close friends and family includes 40 loved ones. The dreams that I never dared to dream were realized.

Milestones in my lives are always bittersweet. I went on to be the first to ever graduate college and obtain a Master's degree.

"Frank, are they here?" I asked as he adjusted my cap and gown.

"No," he said as he rushed me to join my fellow graduates.

My peers around me lined up for the procession and as we walked everyone waved to a loved one, cameras clicked, "thanks mom" placards were raised. I felt myself choke up, thinking of Mami, wishing she was there, wishing my family was there, not just Frank, and I started to cry, feeling all alone.

I'm such an ugly crier. My nose and eyebrows gets red and there's no hiding the fact that I've been crying. I saw Frank rushing to me and surprised, I saw my little nephew, Fabian, right behind him.

"Oh my God, they came!"

Fresh tears of joy trickled out as Silvia and Evi popped out screaming, "Surprise!"

I mistakenly thought I was all alone on this momentous day.

"You silly, of course we came. We just wanted to surprise you."

Most importantly, I went on to give Mami the big church wedding she always wanted. I married Frank straight after college and had a beautiful double wedding with his sister, Luz. Eric, who never dresses up, not even for his own wedding day, wore a handsome black suit and gave me away. It was very special for both of us.

Having Luz by my side throughout all the planning and preparations kept the pain of not having Mami by my side at bay. However, the night before the wedding, when I was alone waiting for the big day, the sadness came and settled in my heart.

"Mami I wish you were here. This is as much for you as for me. I love you."

Life without a mother has been filled with moments when I desperately wished she were there by my side, moments when I needed her advice, guidance, and comfort. I missed out on basic mother and daughter moments, such as having someone teach me how to cook, how to care for my newborn, how to navigate marriage. Luckily, Mami gave me a strong faith and foundation that allowed me to accept and survive life's pain, to carry my crosses with dignity and hope, and God gave me the blessings I needed to rebuild a life far away from my old stoop.

Epilogue

THERE HAVE BEEN so many blessings in my life that I can't begin to count them. My mother was my foundation, and I thank God everyday for giving me to her. She gave me my confidence, my faith, and my survival skills. Not every mother can open herself up so freely and candidly to let her daughter in. She raised six wonderful children that she would be very proud of.

We all got out in our own way. None of us are much of a drinker, drinking on such rare occasions and so minimally that we're barely can be described as social drinkers. I can only speak for myself, but I have never been intoxicated in my entire life, and I'm pretty sure it's the same for my sisters. We all learned the danger of alcoholism and stayed quite clear of it. Just a whiff of alcohol in people's breath sends me back in time, making me horribly tense and uncomfortable. Additionally, none of us have ever been involved with the law, abhorring any kind of unethical behavior, most especially stealing!

After a drug dealer stormed into Silvia's apartment and put a gun to her head looking for her husband, she took her little girl and her pregnant self out of Hartford and started over. She divorced and remarried a wonderful man. She went back to school and obtained her Bachelor's Degree in Engineering. She created a wonderful family, career, and life for herself. Her two girls, Natasha and Tiffany, also went on to college, firmly ending the cycle of high school dropouts.

Eric left early while Mami was alive. He didn't finish high school. At 18 years old, after the adoption of his son, he had enough. He packed his car, took off with a friend, and started a new life in Oklahoma where he knew no one. His greatest gift has been taking in family members and friends, providing a stable home environment to those who need it. He always extended an open hand to anyone wishing to start over. He has a wonderful son, Eros, has raised three other step and foster sons, and eventually met Philip, his first-born son. Like me, he places a strong emphasis on family and faith.

Losing Mami at 14 years old was especially hard for Rose because it also meant simultaneously losing her friends and family and starting over in a whole new state during a very vulnerable age. She lived with Eric but desperately missed Connecticut and her family. Thus, she returned back to Connecticut only to come to the realization that Oklahoma was a better place for her. She went on to graduate high school, marry, and raise two wonderful boys, Joshua and Jacob, who are still attending college.

Evi's path has been a difficult one. She didn't share much of what's in this memoir as she struggled with her own reality. She is an incredible, hard-working woman who too often fails to see her own self-worth and wonderful qualities.

She is strong and has raised three children, Fabian, Dionne, and Ivan. I'm very proud of her kind heart, her generous spirit, and her accomplishments. She is truly a survivor.

As for me, I've shared a happy 31-year history with my husband along with my two girls, Elyssa and Raquel, and grandchildren. We created the stable, loving family that I always craved.

Growing up, we were always the guests at others' family gatherings, enjoying others' traditions, never having our own. I always yearned for my own, and God blessed me with my new extended family, The Mejia Family. My *suegra*, may she rest in peace, was the kindest most loving mother-in-law and grandmother that anyone could have. We shared a special bond. Her constant, genuine joy of life and her generosity was an inspiration for me. My *suegro* was the first father figure that I have ever known. I love him dearly. His quiet strength and intelligence means a lot to me, who never knew the love of a father. I consider all my in-laws as brothers, sisters, uncles, cousins. My family has grown so big that my only wish is to have a dining room where I could accomodate them all in!

They do not know much of my past, so they have no way of knowing how much I dreamed of such healthy, loving family gatherings. Together we have been able to give our children many happy memories filled with special family moments. Be it camping trips, shared vacations, holidays or Sunday dinners, this next generation has known the power of family, love, rituals, and, most importantly, stability. Thank you to my Mejia Family for their loving inclusion of my entire family.

Being a Catholic, I believe we must always be people of hope. Thus, I share my story with young people so that they may always hold on to hope. I tell them how at 15 years old, sitting on the stoop in the project, there was no way that I ever envision myself traveling throughout the United States and abroad, including China, the furthest from Charter Oak Terrace that I could ever had imagined. My imagination would never had conjured up the strings of prominent individuals that I have been fortunate to meet, such as Barack Obama, Shaquille O'Neal, Venus and Serena Williams, Maya Angelou, Emeril Lagasse and others. My imagination was not big enough. Therefore, they must hold on to hope even in their darkest moments.

Mami's life taught me how to make careful choices and how to appreciate every blessing in my life. Furthermore, every day is a gift that should not be squandered. I believe life is a series of memories, both good and bad. Therefore, we need to strive to make as many good memories as possible, not only for ourselves but for those whose lives we touch. And we need to never let bad memories consume us. Rather, we should take them as opportunities to learn and grow. These memories will forge us into the person we become, so we should let them make us stronger, better people.

For me, Jesus was my strength and my role model. I thank Him for holding me in His loving hands. I think of the

Bible story where Jesus is sleeping on the boat, while His disciples are frightened by a turbulent storm. They wake Jesus up saying, "Teacher, do You not care that we are perishing?" And He got up and rebuked the wind and said to the sea, "Hush, be still." And the wind died down and it became perfectly calm. And He said to them, "Why are you afraid? Do you still have no faith?" (Mark 4:38-41). I believe that through faith in God, we will find that He will calm the storms that we are sure to encounter.

About the Author

ELIZABETH MEJIA HAS a Masters in Educational Leadership from the University of Connecticut. Her undergraduate degree was in Sociology and Social Work. She spent fifteen years working with battered women and addressing women's issues. With a commitment to help youth similarly break the cycle of poverty, she went on to serve as Executive Director of Communities In Schools of Miami, an affiliate of the largest stay-in-school non-profit organization dedicated to keeping students at risk of academic failure in school and achieving in life (www.cismiami.org). She was a delegate for the state of Connecticut at the Women's World Conference in Beijing.

Mrs. Mejia, a strong Catholic and feminist, serves as a motivational speaker for school groups, church retreats for youth and women, and in community special events. She is a trainer on multiple topics covering gender, cultural, and communication issues. She has won several awards including the Mayor's Pioneer Award and the Movers and Shakers Award.

She is married to Francisco Mejia and has two daughters, Elyssa and Raquel, and two grandchildren, Isabella and Nicolas, and hopes to have more. <u>Life From The Stoop</u> is her first novel.

Mrs. Mejia enjoys reading, photography, drawing, and traveling. She is an active member of her parish. For over 20 years she has served as a Catechist, living her commitment to bring hope, love, and faith to the next generation.

Prayer of St. Francis

Lord, make me an instrument of Thy peace;
where there is hatred, let me sow love;
where there is injury, pardon;
where there is doubt, faith;
where there is despair, hope;
where there is darkness, light;
and where there is sadness, joy.

O Divine Master,
grant that I may not so much seek to be consoled
as to console;
to be understood, as to understand;
to be loved, as to love;
for it is in giving that we receive,
it is in pardoning that we are pardoned,
and it is in dying that we are born to Eternal Life.

Amen.

Made in the USA
San Bernardino, CA
21 February 2015